THE FABER BOOK OF
20TH-CENTURY GERMAN POEMS

THE FABER BOOK OF
20th-Century German Poems

edited by
MICHAEL HOFMANN

faber and faber

First published in 2005
by Faber and Faber Limited
3 Queen Square London WC1N 3AU
Published in the United States by Faber and Faber Inc.
an affiliate of Farrar, Straus and Giroux LLC, New York

Photoset by RefineCatch Ltd, Bungay, Suffolk
Printed in England by Mackays of Chatham plc, Chatham, Kent

A CIP record for this book
is available from the British Library

ISBN 0−571−19703−5

2 4 6 8 10 9 7 5 3 1

Contents

[xi]

CHRISTIAN MORGENSTERN
1871–1914

Night Song of the Fish

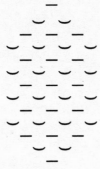

(The deepest German poem)

Introduction

Who had the best poets in the twentieth century? For their size of population, the Irish and the Poles, absolutely, without hesitation. And under open rules? Well, then it's more like the usual suspects, the Americans and the Russians, the Spanish (particularly if you throw in Latin America) – and (beefed up by the Austrians and the Swiss, and a few Czechs and Balts and Romanians) the Germans. I don't think I'm being biased here, except inasmuch as I am able to read the stuff at all. If you're a monoglot in English, you have to struggle mightily to make your Mercator look any better adjusted or more adequately representative than the famous *New Yorker* map of the States. ('Do you mean *foreign* poetry?' exclaims a coiled, repugnant Larkin, asked if he read poetry in translation. As if English poetry in (English!) translation might be acceptable.) To answer the question fairly and properly, you'd have to be a thoroughgoing polyglot; and I'm only a bi-glot. But here's my case anyway.

Rilke, first – whatever else one thinks of him – is at least as good a poet as there has ever been, in point of skill, originality and expression. Brecht, it can be argued, took poetry into the twentieth century. He is even, perhaps, its single most crucial figure; certainly, he would be my choice. That notion was first suggested to me by Daniel Weissbort's brilliant collection of the poetry of World War II, Holocaust, Diaspora, and totalitarian division of Europe, *The Poetry of Survival*, which begins with Brecht. Where now, I've come to think, without Brecht, would there have been poetry as a living counter-force in socio-political reality, where else would the poetry of dissent and fear and protest and rebuke and pleasure have ever begun? Unlike, say, T. S. Eliot or Paul Valery or Garcia Lorca, the idea of Brecht is heartening and inspiring even if you have never read him. He represents utility, and private opposition; 'seid Sand, nicht das Öl im Getriebe der Welt', 'be sand, not oil, in the machinery of the world', as Günter Eich famously and Brecht-ishly said. And if you have read him, I'm sure that with the *ur*-cool of his 'my brother Shelley' *schtick*, and his great 'Motto' ('In the dark times/Will there also be singing?/Yes, there will also be singing/About the dark times.'), his example has made poetry more possible anywhere in the world. If I were a poet in Asia or Africa or Latin America, he is the one 'old world' poet I would go to. He synthesized, improbably, Kipling, Rimbaud, Waley, the Bible and later Horace to make something utterly and radically new. The prevailing British view of him as an arid theorist of drama (you keep the house-lights on, there's no proper acting, and someone writes things down on a blackboard), and the author of a few baffling but conniving plays, excruciatingly boring but now happily debunked, is as bad and thoroughgoing a misrepresentation as any ever perpetrated.

Gottfried Benn, his great counter-pole, and for thirty or forty years the other great German poet (they both died in the summer of 1956, Brecht in East Berlin, Benn in West Berlin), is one of the consummate poets of the century: the poet of private griefs and musics, of monologue, of fascination. What all the mid-century American poets – Lowell, Bishop, Jarrell, Berryman, Roethke, Snodgrass – half-officially set themselves to be, 'heartbreaking,' Benn simply is. There is no one harder, and no one softer. Both Brecht and Benn, inci-dentally, are depleted in translation. Rilke at times puts up quite a plausible showing – I have sometimes referred to him, derisively, as an American poet (but that's mainly a comment on his adoptedness there) – but the subtlety and elegance of Brecht, and the extraordinary, inspissated jargon-glooms of middle-period Benn are barely possible. There's a near-thirty-year gap between 'Express Train' and 'Chopin' in the present selection, in which Benn wrote things I would certainly have liked to represent, but they are short-lined tightly rhyming octaves of techno-collages. I simply would have had no idea what to do with a line like '*Banane, yes, Banane*', which seems to me great and zany poetry, in equal parts hilarious and gravely majestic. Anyway, there's the basis of a century there. Add on the unaccountable and grievous Celan and Sachs and Bachmann and Inge Müller. Add on Hans Magnus Enzensberger, a contemporary and an observer and a participant like Auden or MacNiece, and also a Renaissance of one. Add on Expressionism – a universal literary movement in one country – add on the strange, state-sponsored, but then, at its best, state-biting poetry of East Germany for the best part of fifty years, and you get something not so much imposing as unexpectedly irresistible.

The next thing about German twentieth-century poetry is how closely it is bound up with Germany's villainous history. Benn – who also wrote formidable and hauntingly beautiful prose – speaks of the generation that tramped to war with Rilke's '*Wer spricht von Sieg? Überstehn ist alles.*' – 'Who speaks of victory? Surviving is all.' – on their lips. Quite a few of the poets died in the war, or were left permanently affected (Stadler; Trakl; van Hoddis); Benn himself, a medical doctor, was at HQ in Brussels during the First World War, and was with the Army again in the Second (he was compiling statistics on suicide), describing it as 'the aristocratic form of emigration'. The end of World War II is marked by Ernst Jandl's poem – one of the best and most widely known 'concrete poems' there are. Celan and Nelly Sachs wrote obliquely and more straightforwardly about the death camps; Bobrowski was first inspired to write by the Russian landscape he saw as a prisoner-of-war; Eich wrote about being a prisoner of the Americans. Theodor Adorno's – again – vastly well-known remark about poetry being impossible after Auschwitz drew an oblique reply from Brecht, which drew a more direct one from Celan, and – a little like poetry in Poland (Herbert and Rozewicz) – a bitter and cleansed and haunted poetry sprang up again in Germany in the post-War years, with the 'Gruppe '47' and others. (Those football players of the 'Gruppe '47', as Celan, the unco-optable individualist, witheringly said; but I have to say, mostly they meant well, and did good.)

The false prospectus of 'really existent Socialism' was increasingly criticized in the East (there was an uprising in '54, anticipating that in Hungary in '56, which had to be brutally put down); Brecht, who had sworn never to do anything to harm the cause of Communism, didn't publish or otherwise circulate poems like 'Changing the Wheel' or 'The Solution', but he was at least moved to write them. Meanwhile, the horrid materialism of the 'Economic Miracle' and the 'fake Fifties' (Grass's phrase) was attacked in the West, by Enzensberger and others. In the Sixties, the Federal Republic (West Germany) came increasingly under American influence, Pop culture; Rolf Dieter Brinkmann translated Frank O'Hara and got himself run over in Soho, on Old Compton Street. The more left-wing writers – Germany's *soixante-huitards* – decided that poetry and literature in general were hopelessly bourgeois, and gave them up; after a time, most of them came back. In the East, there was almost a new natural career progression as writers began, wrote critically of the state, and found themselves shunted off to the West (Wolf Biermann's was the most celebrated case, in November 1976, but this relatively discreet and unpleasantly effective practice continued for at least a decade). As in Brecht's time, a word or phrase could still have immense carry: I think of two titles: Uwe Kolbe's

'*Hineingeboren*' ('Born into it' – i.e., East Germany), and Durs Grünbein's '*Grauzone Morgens*' ('Mornings in the Grayzone' – i.e., once again, East Germany). As the century ended, a reunified country was looking at itself and its neighbours in new ways (Grass; Grünbein; Göritz).

The other thing that maybe separates German poets from those of other countries is how many of them do other things. There were painters like Klee, Schwitters, Arp, and Grosz. Christoph Meckel and Günter Grass are very accomplished graphic artists. Brecht and Heiner Müller and now Durs Grünbein are all playwrights. Benn was a doctor, and Trakl a pharmacist. Grass, evidently, is far better known as a novelist; but Werfel also had a huge bestseller with *The Song of Bernadette*, while Rilke, Brecht, Bobrowski, Bachmann, Born, Braun, Krüger and Beyer have all written novels; Günter Eich was an admired writer of radio plays; Celan translated poetry from Russian, French, English, and other languages; Bartsch and Müller adapted Shakespeare; Enzensberger and Sartorius, each in their generation, compiled anthologies of world poetry, Krüger is the most important German publisher. Benn and Enzensberger and Grünbein are all prolific essayists. I enumerate this, in such detail, to demonstrate how much the poets here are 'in the world'; 'pure poets' and ivory tower-ites are elsewhere.

Possibly related to this is a streak of rebelliousness in many of the poems against what one might think of as a German temperament. It is the reverence to America of George Grosz (who once, as a child, copied out a Fenimore Cooper novel by hand), or to Poland of Johannes Bobrowski's 'Report'; it is the startling low comedy of Rilke's tailor-king (in a spectacular translation by Don Paterson) and Enzensberger's beautiful praise ('precise/ and peculiarly cheerful' – the antithesis of anything *typisch deutsch*) for William Carlos Williams; it is Günter Grass's worry about the standard-issue copy of Hölderlin in the soldier's knapsack, and Rainer Kunze's about the tyrannical imposition of a more than literal 'Beethoven'; it is the persistent concreteness of Brecht ('truth is always concrete' was one of his great sayings, which he kept appropriately pinned to the wall), and the moving simplicity of Celan's very late – and impossible – do-it to himself, that he 'learn to live'. It is the undiminished truculence of Heiner Müller and Volker Braun – even after the '*Wende*' and the re-absorption of the East. It is Eich's 'I have always loved nettles,/ and only now learned/ of their usefulness' and part of Pastior's wonderful portmanteau, 'riennevapluperfect'. It is the scepticism of Brecht's '*Und nach uns wird kommen: nichts nennenswertes*', in 'Of Poor B.B.': 'And after us there will come: nothing worth talking about' in Michael Hamburger's translation – a line, incidentally, which is echoed at the end of Enzensberger's 'Fetish' ('*und nicht weiter/ nennenswert*' in the original) and more explicitly cited in Volker Braun's 'O Chicago! O Dialectic!' That sort of moody or whimsical or sophisticated rejection is of course explicitly against the whole tenor of Rilke's Ninth Duino Elegy, in which he makes poets responsible for naming and telling.

In a wider way, it is an inevitable – but also a deliberately fostered – aspect of the selection that many of the poems here appeal to, or celebrate, or attempt to take forward the example of other poets, both within and beyond Germany, within and beyond the limits of this book. Hence Lasker-Schüler's portrait of Grosz (a former lover), Benn's Shakespeare, Bobrowski's Trakl, Kunert's Koeppen, Heiner Müller's Brecht, Kunze's Bobrowski, Bartsch's Enzensberger (with its allusions to the latter's great, and unfortunately not very excerptible, long poem, *The Sinking of the Titanic*),

Sartorius's Cavafy, Krüger's Ernst Meister, even, in its utterly elliptical way, Grünbein's Vallejo.

This book aims to be at once readable, objective and unfair. There are inevitable omissions and distortions – on the whole, I don't want to apologize for them. I didn't want to leave out great poets (Rilke, Brecht) just because one can find them elsewhere, or great poems either ('Orpheus. Eurydice. Hermes', which Joseph Brodsky nominated as possibly the greatest poem of the century; 'Poor B.B.' and 'To Those Born Later'; 'Morgue'; 'Inventory'; 'Deathfugue' – in John Felstiner's challenging retro-translation). I tried to take seriously the anthology-as-island. Therefore, one way or another, the poems here are meant to travel: they are great in the original, or good in English, or there is nothing like them in either language, or in many cases perhaps all three. When I first read through what I had assembled, it seemed to me that it was both true to itself and not unassimilable to an English readership. Historically, I don't think twentieth-century German poetry has had much effect on English and American poetry, except, in a shallow and mistaken way, Celan and Rilke. But there is much that might. Jakob Van Hoddis has a slapstick feel – like a Feininger drawing – on top of Expressionism's end-of-the-world aura. Robert Lowell's Werfel translation sounds altogether more like his own poetry of fifteen years later (and indeed contains a phrase that appeared in *Life Studies*). Hans Magnus Enzensberger's 'At Thirty-Three' and 'The Holiday' both come out of a 1979 book called *Die Furie des Verschwindens*, which, had it been in English, would surely have made even greater waves. I can imagine the delight of Charles Simic (whom Enzensberger has translated into German) at the asperities of Günter Eich, or the drastic economy of Inge Müller. Benn's poems from the 1940s read like fifty years later. Many of the works here are both international and English – and that at a time when too few English poems are international.

I would like to thank Bill Donahue, Barbara Honrath, Hauke Hückstädt, Ludwig Krapf and Eliot Weinberger, for their respective *empfindlich* bits of help. 'Like being handed a lantern, or a spiked stick,' as the poet said, or rather, the poets said. Also to the example of my friends, Stephen Romer and Jamie McKendrick. Once upon a time, we all set off together at the same time. I stand in their slipstream.

Michael Hofmann
Feldafing, September 2004

THE FABER BOOK OF
20TH-CENTURY GERMAN POEMS

George Grosz

Sometimes coloured tears play
In his ashen eyes.

He is forever encountering funeral processions
Which scatter his dragonflies.

He is superstitious –
Born under a bad star –

His writing rains,
His drawings: gloomy alphabets.

His people are bloated,
As though they'd long lain in rivers,

Mysterious missing persons with fish-mouths
And mouldering souls.

His silver fingers
Are five dreamy undertakers.

Nowhere is there a light in his lost *Märchen*,
But he remains a boy at heart,

A Fenimore Cooper hero;
On first-name terms with a tribe of Indians.

Apart from them, he hates everyone,
They bring him bad luck.

But George Grosz loves his fate
Like a trusty enemy.

And his sadness is Dionysian,
Black champagne his plaints.

No one knows where he came from;
I know where he ends up.

He is a sea with a dim moon above it,
His god is only playing dead.

Michael Hofmann

RAINER MARIA RILKE
1875–1926

Autumn Day

Lord, it is time. The summer was too long.
Lay now thy shadow over the sundials,
and on the meadows let the winds blow strong.

Bid the last fruit to ripen on the vine;
allow them still two friendly southern days
to bring them to perfection and to force
the final sweetness in the heavy wine.

Who has no house now will not build him one.
Who is alone now will be long alone,
will waken, read, and write long letters
and through the barren pathways up and down
restlessly wander when dead leaves are blown.

C. F. MacIntyre

The Spanish Dancer

The audience in the cup of her hand,
she is a struck match: sparks,
darting tongues, and then the white flare
of phosphorus and the dance ignites
a charm of fire, uncoiling, spreading fast.

And suddenly she is all flame.

She is brazen: glancing round and shamelessly
setting her hair alight, turning her dress
to a seething inferno, from which she stretches

long white arms, and castanets, like rattlesnakes
woken, startled to their ratcheting and clack.

And just as quick, as if constricted
by the sheath of fire, she gathers it up
and casts it off in one high gesture,
and looks down: it lies there raging on the ground,
shed flame stubbornly alive.
Radiant, chin tilted in salute, she dispatches it
with a steely fusillade of feet:
stamps it, pounds it, stamps it out.

Robin Robertson

Blue Hydrangea

Like the green that cakes in a pot of paint,
these leaves are dry, dull and rough
behind this billow of blooms whose blue
is not their own but reflected from far away
in a mirror dimmed by tears and vague,
as if it wished them to disappear again
the way, in old blue writing paper,
yellow shows, then violet and gray;

a washed-out color as in children's clothes
which, no longer worn, no more can happen to:
how much it makes you feel a small life's brevity.
But suddenly the blue shines quite renewed
within one cluster, and we can see
a touching blue rejoice before the green.

William Gass

Before Summer Rain

Suddenly, from all the green around you,
something – you don't know what – has disappeared;
you feel it creeping closer to the window,
in total silence. From the nearby wood

you hear the urgent whistling of a plover,
reminding you of someone's *Saint Jerome*:
so much solitude and passion come
from that one voice, whose fierce request the downpour

will grant. The walls, with their ancient portraits, glide
away from us, cautiously, as though
they weren't supposed to hear what we are saying.

And reflected on the faded tapestries now:
the chill, uncertain sunlight of those long
childhood hours when you were so afraid.

Stephen Mitchell

Orpheus. Eurydice. Hermes

That was the so unfathomed mine of souls.
And they, like silent veins of silver ore,
were winding through its darkness. Between roots
welled up the blood that flows on to mankind,
like blocks of heavy porphyry in the darkness.
Else there was nothing red.

But there were rocks
and ghostly forests. Bridges over voidness
and that immense, grey, unreflecting pool
that hung above its so far distant bed

[7]

like a grey rainy sky above a landscape.
And between meadows, soft and full of patience,
appeared the pale strip of the single pathway,
like a long line of linen laid to bleach.

And on this single pathway they approached.

In front the slender man in the blue mantle,
gazing in dumb impatience straight before him.
His steps devoured the way in mighty chunks
they did not pause to chew; his hands were hanging,
heavy and clenched, out of the falling folds,
no longer conscious of the lightsome lyre,
the lyre which had grown into his left
like twines of rose into a branch of olive.
It seemed as though his senses were divided:
for, while his sight ran like a dog before him,
turned round, came back, and stood, time and again,
distant and waiting, at the path's next turn,
his hearing lagged behind him like a smell.
It seemed to him at times as though it stretched
back to the progress of those other two
who should be following up this whole ascent.
Then once more there was nothing else behind him
but his climb's echo and his mantle's wind.
He, though, assured himself they still were coming;
said it aloud and heard it die away.
They still were coming, only they were two
that trod with fearful lightness. If he durst
but once look back (if only looking back
were not undoing of this whole enterprise
still to be done), he could not fail to see them,
the two light-footers, following him in silence:

The god of faring and of distant message,
the travelling-hood over his shining eyes,
the slender wand held out before his body,
the wings around his ankles lightly beating,
and in his left hand, as entrusted, *her*.

She, so belov'd, that from a single lyre
more mourning rose than from all women-mourners, –
that a whole world of mourning rose, wherein
all things were once more present: wood and vale
and road and hamlet, field and stream and beast, –
and that around this world of mourning turned,
even as around the other earth, a sun
and a whole silent heaven full of stars,
a heaven of mourning with disfigured stars: –
she, so beloved.

But hand in hand now with that god she walked,
her paces circumscribed by lengthy shroudings,
uncertain, gentle, and without impatience.
Wrapt in herself, like one whose time is near,
she thought not of the man who went before them,
nor of the road ascending into life.
Wrapt in herself she wandered. And her deadness
was filling her like fullness.
Full as a fruit with sweetness and with darkness
was she with her great death, which was so new
that for the time she could take nothing in.

She had attained a new virginity
and was intangible; her sex had closed
like a young flower at the approach of evening,
and her pale hands had grown so disaccustomed
to being a wife, that even the slim god's

endlessly gentle contact as he led her
disturbed her like a too great intimacy.

Even now she was no longer that blonde woman
who'd sometimes echoed in the poet's poems,
no longer the broad couch's scent and island,
nor yonder man's possession any longer.

She was already loosened like long hair,
and given far and wide like fallen rain,
and dealt out like a manifold supply.

She was already root.
And when, abruptly,
the god had halted her and, with an anguished
outcry, outspoke the words: He has turned round! —
she took in nothing, and said softly: Who?

But in the distance, dark in the bright exit,
someone or other stood, whose countenance
was indistinguishable. Stood and saw
how, on a strip of pathway between meadows,
with sorrow in his look, the god of message
turned silently to go behind the figure
already going back by that same pathway,
its paces circumscribed by lengthy shroudings,
uncertain, gentle, and without impatience.

J. B. Leishman

The King of Munster

His Highness had been scalped;
his crown, now too big, pinned
his lugs down like a whelp's.

From time to time, the sound
of hunger-stoked alarm
would reach them on the wind.
He sat, to keep it warm,
upon his stitching-hand,
fat-arsed, bald and snivelling.
He knew himself unmanned;
the king in him was shrivelling
and he couldn't get a stand.

Don Paterson

'Exposed on the cliffs of the heart'

Exposed on the cliffs of the heart. Look, how tiny down
   there,
look: the last village of words and, higher,
(but how tiny) still one last
farmhouse of feeling. Can you see it?
Exposed on the cliffs of the heart. Stoneground
under your hands. Even here, though,
something can bloom; on a silent cliff-edge
an unknowing plant blooms, singing, into the air.
But the one who knows? Ah, he began to know
and is quiet now, exposed on the cliffs of the heart.
While, with their full awareness,
many sure-footed mountain animals pass
or linger. And the great sheltered bird flies, slowly
circling, around the peak's pure denial.– But
without a shelter, here on the cliffs of the heart. . . .

Stephen Mitchell

[11]

The Ninth Elegy

Why, when this span of life might be fleeted away
as laurel, a little darker than all
the surrounding green, with tiny waves on the border
of every leaf (like the smile of a wind): – oh, why
have to be human, and, shunning Destiny,
long for Destiny? . . .

                           Not because happiness really
exists, that precipitate profit of imminent loss.
Not out of curiosity, not just to practise the heart,
that could still be there in laurel. . . .
But because being here is much, and because all this
that's here, so fleeting, seems to require us and strangely
concerns us. Us the most fleeting of all. Just once,
everything, only for once. Once and no more. And we, too,
once. And never again. But this
having been once, though only once,
having been once on earth—can it ever be cancelled?

And so we keep pressing on and trying to perform it,
trying to contain it within our simple hands,
in the more and more crowded gaze, in the speechless heart.
Trying to become it. To give it to whom? We'd rather
hold on to it all for ever . . . But into the other relation,
what, alas! do we carry across? Not the beholding we've
    here
slowly acquired, and no here occurrence. Not one.
Sufferings, then. Above all, the hardness of life,
the long experience of love; in fact,
purely untellable things. But later,
under the stars, what use? the more deeply untellable stars?
Yet the wanderer too doesn't bring from mountain to valley

[12]

a handful of earth, of for all untellable earth, but only
a word he has won, pure, the yellow and blue
gentian. Are we, perhaps, *here* just for saying: House,
Bridge, Fountain, Gate, Jug, Fruit tree, Window, –
possibly: Pillar, Tower? . . . but for *saying*, remember,
oh, for such saying as never the things themselves
hoped so intensely to be. Is not the secret purpose
of this sly Earth, in urging a pair of lovers,
just to make everything leap with ecstasy in them?
Threshold : what does it mean
to a pair of lovers, that they should be wearing their own
worn threshold a little, they too, after the many before,
before the many to come, . . . as a matter of course!

Here is the time for the Tellable, *here* is its home.
Speak and proclaim. More than ever
things we can live with are falling away, for that
which is oustingly taking their place is an imageless act.
Act under crusts, that will readily split as soon
as the doing within outgrows them and takes a new outline.
Between the hammers lives on
our heart, as between the teeth
the tongue, which, in spite of all,
still continues to praise.

Praise this world to the Angel, not the untellable: you
can't impress him with the splendour you've felt; in the
   cosmos
where he more feelingly feels you're only a novice. So show
   him
some simple thing, refashioned by age after age,
till it lives in our hands and eyes as a part of ourselves.
Tell him *things*. He'll stand more astonished: as you did
beside the roper in Rome or the potter in Egypt.

[13]

Show him how happy a thing can be, how guileless and
    ours;
how even the moaning of grief purely determines on form,
serves as a thing, or dies into a thing,—to escape
to a bliss beyond the fiddle. These things that live on
    departure
understand when you praise them: fleeting, they look for
rescue through something in us, the most fleeting of all.
Want us to change them entirely, within our invisible
    hearts,
into – oh, endlessly – into ourselves! Whosoever we are.

Earth, is it not just this that you want : to arise
invisibly in us? Is not your dream
to be one day invisible? Earth! invisible!
What is your urgent command, if not transformation?
Earth, you darling, I will! Oh, believe me, you need
no more of your spring-times to win me over : a single one,
ah, one, is already more than my blood can endure.
Beyond all names I am yours, and have been for ages.
You were always right, and your holiest inspiration
is Death, that friendly Death.
Look, I am living. On what? Neither childhood nor future
are growing less. . . . Supernumerous existence
wells up in my heart.

J. B. Leishman and Stephen Spender

The Unicorn

This, then, is the beast that has never actually been:
not having seen one, they prized in any case
its perfect poise, its throat, the straightforward gaze
it gave them back – so straightforward, so serene.

Since it had never been, it was all the more
unsullied. And they allowed it such latitude
that, in a clearing in the wood,
it raised its head as if its essence shrugged off mere

existence. They brought it on, not with oats or corn,
but with the chance, however slight,
that it might come into its own. This gave it such strength

that from its brow there sprang a horn. A single horn.
Only when it met a maiden's white with white
would it be bodied out in her, in her mirror's full length.

Paul Muldoon

Water

Water,
topped by waves,
topped by a boat,
topped by a woman,
topped by a man.

Harriet Watts

On Crossing the Rhine Bridge at Cologne by night

The express train gropes and thrusts its way through
  darkness. Not a star is out.
The whole world's nothing but a mine-road the night has
  railed about
In which at times conveyors of blue light tear sudden
  horizons: fiery sphere
Of arc-lamps, roofs and chimneys, steaming, streaming –
  for seconds only clear,
And all is black again. As though we drove into Night's
  entrails to the seam.
Now lights reel into view . . . astray, disconsolate and lonely
  . . . more . . . and gather . . . and densely gleam.
Skeletons of grey housefronts are laid bare, grown pale in
  the twilight, dead—something must happen . . . O
  heavily
I feel it weigh on my brain. An oppression sings in the
  blood. Then all at once the ground resounds like the sea:
And royally upborne we fly through air from darkness
  wrested, high up above the river. O curve of the million
  lights, mute guard at the sight
Of whose flashing parade the waters go roaring down.
  Endless line presenting arms by night!
Surging on like torches! Joyful! Salute of ships over the blue
  sea! Star-jewelled, festive array!
Teeming, bright-eyed urged on! Till where the town with its
  last houses sees its guest away.

[17]

And then the long solitudes. Bare banks. And Silence.
Night. Reflection. Self-questioning. Communion. And
ardor outward-flowing.
To the end that blesses. To conception's rite. To pleasure's
consummation. To prayer. To the sea. To self's undoing.

Michael Hamburger

GOTTFRIED BENN
1886–1956

from Morgue

I LITTLE ASTER

A drowned truck-driver was propped on the slab.
Someone had stuck a lavender aster
between his teeth.
As I cut out the tongue and the palate,
through the chest
under the skin,
with my long knife,
I must have touched the flower, for it slid
into the brain lying next.
I packed it into the cavity of the chest
among the excelsior
as it was sewn up.
Drink yourself full in your vase!
Rest softly,
little aster!

II LOVELY CHILDHOOD

The mouth of a girl who had long lain among the reeds
    looked gnawed away.
As the breast was cut open, the gullet showed full of holes.
Finally in a cavity below the diaphragm
a nest of young rats was discovered.
One little sister lay dead.
The others thrived on liver and kidneys,
drank the cold blood and
enjoyed a lovely childhood here.

And sweet and swift came their death also:
They were all thrown into the water together.
Oh, how the little muzzles squeaked!

Babette Deutsch

Night Café

824: Lives and Loves of Women.
The cello takes a quick drink. The flute
belches expansively for three beats: good old dinner.
The timpani is desperate to get to the end of his thriller.

Mossed teeth and pimple face
wave to incipient stye.

Greasy hair
talks to open mouth with adenoids
Faith Love Hope round her neck.

Young goitre has a crush on saddlenose.
He treats her to onetwothree beers.

Sycosis brings carnations
to melt the heart of double chin.

B flat minor: the 35th Sonata.
Two eyes yell:
stop hosing the blood of Chopin round the room
for that rabble to slosh around in!
Enough! Hey, Gigi! –

The door melts away: a woman.
Dry desert. Canaanite tan.
Chaste. Concavities. A scent accompanies her,
                              less a scent

than a sweet pressure of the air
against my brain.

An obesity waddles after.

Michael Hofmann

Express Train

Brown as cognac. Brown as leaves. Red-brown. Malayan
   yellow.
Express train Berlin-Trelleborg and the Baltic Sea resorts.

Flesh, that went naked.
Tanned to the very lips by the sea.
Deeply ripe, for Grecian pleasure.
And yearning for the scythe: how long the summer seems!

Almost the end of the ninth month already!

Stubble and the last almond thirst in us.
Unfoldings, the blood, the weariness,
The nearness of dahlias confuses us.

Man-brown hurls itself upon woman-brown:

A woman is something for a night.
And if it was good, for the next night too!
Oh, and then again this being by oneself!
These silences! This letting oneself drift!

A woman is something with fragrance.
Unspeakable. Dissolve. Reseda.
In her the south, shepherd and sea.
On every slope a pleasure lies.

Woman-light-brown reels towards man-dark-brown:

Hold me, dear; I'm falling.
I'm so weary at the neck.
Oh, this feverish sweet
Last fragrance blown from the gardens.

Michael Hamburger

Chopin

Not much of a conversationalist,
ideas weren't his strong suit,
ideas miss the point,
when Delacroix expounded his theories
it made him nervous, he for his part
could offer no explanation of the Nocturnes.

A poor lover;
mere shadow in Nohant
where George Sand's children
rejected his attempts
at discipline.

His tuberculosis
took the chronic form,
with repeated bleeding and scarring;
a creeping death,
as opposed to one
in convulsions of agony
or by firing squad:
the piano (Erard) was pushed back against the door
and Delphine Potocka
sang him
a violet song in his last hour.

[22]

He took three pianos with him to England:
Pleyel, Erard, Broadwood,
for twenty guineas
he would give fifteen-minute recitals in the evenings
at the Rothschilds' and the Wellingtons', in Strafford House
to the assembled cummerbunds;
then, dark with fatigue and imminent death,
he went home
to the Square d'Orleans.

Then he burned his sketches
and manuscripts,
didn't want any leftover scraps
betraying him –
at the end he said:
'I have taken my experiment
as far as it was possible for me to go.'

Each finger was to play
to no more than its natural strength,
the fourth being the weakest
(twinned with the middle finger).
At the start, they occupied the keys
of E, F sharp, G sharp, B and C.

Anyone hearing
certain of his Preludes
in country seats or
at altitude,
through open French windows
on the terrace, say, of a sanatorium,
will not easily forget it.

He composed no operas,
no symphonies,

only those tragic progressions
from artistic conviction
and with a small hand.

Michael Hofmann

Little Sweet Face

Little sweet face,
shrunken already in transit,
snowy-, nearly deathly pale,
great outpouring of grief
when you shortly passed
away –

We played together
quite unmindful of our state of development
all looks back and out
cropped,
living, experiencing nothing
outside the charmed circle
of our own noises!

Hobbled – blinkered! But once,
the men beating the olive-trees, obscured by branches,
piles of fruit set to ripen.
Once, wine from the Gulf of Lions
in smoky vaults, accented with sea water.
Or giant eucalypts, 400 feet high,
and the trembling light under their crowns.
Once to Cotroceni –
once only.

Little face
snowflake

always so white
and the blue vein at the temple
Ligurian grape-hyacinth
blue,
musk-scented.

Michael Hofmann

The Evenings of Certain Lives

I

You needn't always be scrubbing the tiles, Hendrickje,

my eye drinks itself,
drinks itself dry –
but then it has no other liquor –
the statue of Buddha over there,
Chinese god of the bosk,
as against a good tot of Hulstkamp,
I ask you!

Never painted a thing
in frost-white or skater's blue
or in Irish green
with the purple flickering out of it –
only my own monotony always –
my coactive shadows –
it's not pleasant
to follow this bent with such distinctness.

Greatness – where?
I take my pencil
and certain things emerge, stand there

on paper, canvas
or similar tinder –

result: bronze Buddha as against hooch –
all those obeisances under indoor plants,
banquet of the dimwit daubers' guild –
give it to the genre painter!

. . . Rattles,
lambs bleating,
transfers,
Flemish, rubenesque,
for small grandchildren –
(likewise idiots! –)

Ah – Hulstkamp –
midpoint of warmth,
center of colors,
my shadow brown –
aura of unshaved bristle round heart and eye –

II

The fire is smoking
– the Swan of Avon blows his nose –
the tree-stumps are wet,
clammy night, emptiness suffused with draughts –
have done with characters,
earth overpopulated
by copious fall of peach, four rosebuds
pro anno –
strewn far and wide,
thrust on the boards
by this hand,

with its wrinkles now,
and its exhausted veins.

All the Ophelias, Juliets
wreathed, silvery, also murderous –
all the soft mouths, the sighs
I manipulated out of them –
the first actresses long since vapor,
rust, lixiviated, rats' pudding –
even the heart's Ariel off to the elements.

The age takes off its Sunday best.
These duke and desperado skulls,
their trains of thought
I drove to the extreme –
my history-making gentlemen
all illiterates of crown and sceptre,
major powers of space,
like flittermouse or paper kite!

Sir Goon recently wrote to me:
'The rest is silence.'
I think I said that myself,
nobody else could have said it,
Dante dead – a great emptiness
between the centuries
up to the quotations from my vocabulary –

but if they were missing,
if all that stuff had never been turned out,
the booths and the gallowtrees, if the bells
had never jingled –:
gaps then? Gaps possibly in the teeth,
but the ape's great jaws
would go on grinding

their emptiness the draughts suffuse –
the tree-stumps are wet,
and the butler snores in his porter dreams.

Christopher Middleton

Fragments

Fragments,
soul flotsam,
coagulates of the twentieth century –

scars – break in flow from the dawn of creation,
the historical religions of five centuries in smithereens,
science: cracks in the Parthenon,
Planck running to Kepler and Kierkegaard
with the fresh murk of his quantum theory –

but there were evenings robed in the colours
of the Almighty, loose, flowing,
incontrovertible in the silence
of their streaming blues,
colour of introverts,
there I sat
hands propped on knees
like a farmer,
quietly nursing my drink
while the labourers played harmonicas –

and others
are driven by inner whorls,
convolutes,
architectonic compressions
or amours.

Crises of expression and spasms of eros:
that's the man of today,
the inside a vacuum,
the continuity of personality
held together by his suit,
which with stout cloth might be good for ten years.

The rest fragments,
mi-voix,
snatches of melody from next door,
Negro spirituals
or Ave Marias.

  Michael Hofmann

Blue Hour

I

I enter the deep blue hour –
here is the landing, the chain shuts behind
and now in the room only carmine on a mouth
and a bowl of late roses – you!

We both know, those words
that we both spoke and often offered others
are of no account and out of place between us:
this is everything and endgame.

Silence has advanced so far
it fills the room and seals it shut
the hour – nothing hoped and nothing suffered –
with its bowl of late roses – you.

II

Your face blurs, is white and fragile,
meanwhile there collects on your mouth
all of desire, the purple and the blossoms
from some ancestral flotsam stock.

You are so pale, I think you might disintegrate
in a snowdrift, in unblooming
deathly white roses, one by one – coral
only on your lips, heavy and like a wound.

You are so soft, you portend something
of happiness, of submersion and danger
in a blue, a deep blue hour
and when it's gone, no one knows if it was.

III

I remind you, you are another's,
what are you doing bearing me these late roses?
You say dreams bleach, hours wander,
what is all this: he and I and you?

'What arises and arouses, it all comes to an end,
what happens – who exactly knows,
the chain falls shut, we are silent in these walls,
and outside is all of space, lofty and dark blue.'

Michael Hofmann

Comme ci, comme ça

There were no Gainsboroughs hanging in my parents'
    house
and no one played Chopin
perfectly philistrous intellectual life
my father had been to the theatre once
in the early century
Wildenbruch's 'Crested Lark'
that was our pabulum
there was nothing else.

All long gone now
grey hearts, grey hair
the garden in Polish hands
the graves *comme ci, comme ça*
but all on the Slavic side
Oder-Neisse Line
inapplicable to the contents of coffins
the children continue to think about them
the spouses too for a while
comme ci, comme ça
till it's time for them to move on
Selah, end of psalm.

Even now in the big city night
café terrace
summer stars
from the next door table
assessments
of hotels in Frankfurt
the ladies frustrated
if their desires had mass
they would each of them weigh twenty stone.

But the electricity in the air! Balmy night
à la travel brochure and
the girls step out of their pictures
improbable lovelies
legs up to here, a waterfall,
their surrender is something one daren't even begin
to contemplate.

Married couples by comparison disappoint,
don't cut it, fail to clear the net,
he smokes, she twists her rings,
worth considering
the whole relationship between marriage and creativity,
stifling or galvanizing.

Questions, questions! Scribbled nictitations
on a summer night,
there were no Gainsboroughs hanging in my parents' house
now everything has gone under
the whole thing, *comme ci, comme ça*,
Selah, end of psalm.

Michael Hofmann

People Met

I have met people who, when asked what their names were,
Apologetically, as if they had no right to claim one's
     attention
Even with an appellation, would answer,
'Miss Vivian,' then add, 'Just like the Christian name';
They wanted to make things easier, no complicated names
Like Popkiss or Umpleby-Dunball –
'Just like the Christian name' – so please do not burden your
     memory!

I have met people who grew up in a single room together with
Parents and four brothers and sisters; they studied by night,
Their fingers in their ears, beside the kitchen range;
They became eminent,
Outwardly beautiful, veritable *grandes dames*, and
Inwardly gentle and active as Nausicaa,
With brows clear as angels' brows.

Often I have asked myself, but found no answer,
Where gentleness and goodness can possibly come from;
Even today I can't tell, and it's time to be gone.

    Christopher Middleton

Listen

Listen, this is what the last evening will be like
when you're still capable of going out: you're smoking your Junos,
quaffing your three pints of Wurzburger Hofbrau
and reading about the UN as reflected in the pages of the *Spiegel*,

you're sitting alone at your little table, the least possible company
beside the radiator, because you crave warmth.
All round you mankind and its mewling,
the couple and their loathsome hound.

That's all you are, you've no house or hill
to call your own, for dreaming in a sunny landscape,
from your birth to this evening
the walls around you were always pretty tightly drawn.

That's all you were, but Zeus and all the immortals,
the great souls, the cosmos and all the suns
were there for you too, spun and fed through you,
that's all you were, finished as begun –
your last evening – good night.

Michael Hofmann

The Demons of the Cities

They wander through the cities night enshrouds:
The cities cower, black, beneath their feet.
Upon their chins like sailors' beards the clouds
Are black with curling smoke and sooty sleet.

On seas of houses their long shadow sways
And snuffs ranked street-lamps out, as with a blow.
Upon the pavement, thick as fog, it weighs,
And gropes from house to house, solid and slow.

With one foot planted on a city square,
The other knee upon a tower, they stand,
And where the black rain falls they rear, with blare
Of quickened Pan's-pipes in a cloud-stormed land.

About their feet circles a ritornelle
With the sad music of the city's sea,
Like a great burying-song. The shrill tones swell
And rumble in the darkness, changefully.

They wander to the stream that, dark and wide,
As a bright reptile with gold-spotted back,
Turns in the lanterned dark from side to side
In its sad dance, while heaven's stare is black.

They lean upon the bridge, darkly agog,
And thrust their hands among the crowds that pass,
Like fauns who perch above a meadow bog
And plunge lean arms into the miry mass.

Now one stands up. He hangs a mask of gloom
Upon the white-cheeked moon. The night, like lead
From the dun heavens, settles as a doom
On houses into pitted darkness fled.

The shoulders of the cities crack. A gleam
Of fire from a roof burst open flies
Into the air. Big-boned, on the top beam
They sit and scream like cats against the skies.

A little room with glimmering shadows billows
Where one in labor shrieks her agony.
Her body lifts gigantic from the pillows.
And the huge devils stand about to see.

She clutches, shaking, at her torture-bed.
With her long shuddering cry the chamber heaves.
Now the fruit comes. Her womb gapes long and red,
And bleeding, for the child's last passage cleaves.

The devils' necks grow like giraffes'. The child
Is born without a head. The mother moans
And holds it. On her back, clammy and wild,
The frog-fingers of fear play, as she swoons.

But vast as giants now the demons loom.
Their horns in fury gore the bleeding skies.
An earthquake thunders in the cities' womb
About their hooves, where flint-struck fires rise.

Babette Deutsch and Avrahm Yarmolinsky

Umbra Vitae

The people on the streets draw up and stare,
While overhead huge portents cross the sky;
Round fanglike towers threatening comets flare,
Death-bearing, fiery-snouted where they fly.

On every roof astrologers abound,
Enormous tubes thrust heavenward; there are
Magicians springing up from underground,
Aslant in darkness, conjuring to a star.

Through night great hordes of suicides are hurled,
Men seeking on their way the selves they've lost;
Crook-backed they haunt all corners of the world,
And with their arms for brooms they sweep the dust.

They are as dust, keep but a little while;
And as they move their hair drops out. They run,
To hasten their slow dying. Then they fall,
And in the open fields lie prone,

But twitch a little still. Beasts of the field
Stand blindly round them, prod with horns
Their sprawling bodies till at last they yield,
Lie buried by the sage-bush, by the thorns.

But all the seas are stopped. Among the waves
The ships hang rotting, scattered, beyond hope.
No current through the water moves,
And all the courts of heaven are locked up.

Trees do not change, the seasons do not change.
Enclosed in dead finality each stands,
And over broken roads lets frigid range
Its palmless thousand-fingered hands.

The dying man sits up, as if to stand,
Just one more word a moment since he cries,
All at once he's gone. Can life so end?
And crushed to fragments are his glassy eyes.

The secret shadows thicken, darkness breaks;
Behind the speechless doors dreams watch and creep.
Burdened by light of dawn the man that wakes
Must rub from grayish eyelids leaden sleep.

Christopher Middleton

The Dead Girl in the Water

Masts tower against the sea-wall's grey
like a charred forest in the red of dawn,
black as slag. Where dead water turns
towards warehouses rotted with decay.

Returning tides beat with a muffled shock
along the quay. The city's nightfall slime
drifts like a skin of white upon the stream
to brush against the steamer in the dock.

Dust, fruit, paper clot and drift and spread
where pipes spill scourings from the city's swamp.
A white ball-dress comes now, in bloated pomp
a bare throat and a face as white as lead.

The body wallows up, inflates the dress
as if it were a white ship in the wind.
The lifeless eyes stare up, enormous, blind,
into a sky of cloud-pink rosiness.

The lilac water gently rocks and swells,
the wake stirred by the water-rats, who man

the white ship. Now it drifts serenely on,
writhing with grey heads and with sable pelts.

In bliss the dead girl rides the outward draw
of wind and tide, her swollen belly heaving,
big, hollowed out, all that the rats are leaving.
It murmurs like a grotto as they gnaw.

She drifts into the ocean. Neptune hails
her from a wreck as the sea gulps her down
and she falls fathoms into depths of green
to rest her fill in the plump kraken's coils.

Anthony Hasler

Poet à la Mode

Autumn is here.
The autumn poet creeps
through the red land
enshrouded in his heavy cloak,
its draping folds a poem to the eye.
And with face drear enough to die
he takes with white and slender hand
the golden pencil from
behind his ear.

Then he sits down in the damp grass –
certainly not, he mustn't let
his patent-leather shoes get wet.
No, huddled on a bench,
he shivers at the pinch
of winter's chill approach,
and watches the dead-weary sun
limping towards its tomb;

at last he scrawls his drivel down
on paper from Japan
stinking of the roses' latest bloom,
not seeing that the children
flying their kites
high in the blue autumn day
are vying with my dear old sun
to mock the wretched parasite.

Anthony Hasler

JAKOB VAN HODDIS
1887–1942

End of the World

The bourgeois' hat flies off his pointed head,
the air re-echoes with a screaming sound.
Tilers plunge from roofs and hit the ground,
and seas are rising round the coasts (you read).

The storm is here, crushed dams no longer hold,
the savage seas come inland with a hop.
The greater part of people have a cold.
Off bridges everywhere the railroads drop.

Christopher Middleton

GEORG TRAKL
1887–1914

Dream of Evil

A gong's brown-golden tones no longer loud –
A lover wakes in chambers growing dimmer,
His cheek near flames that in the window glimmer.
Upon the stream flash rigging, mast and shroud.

A monk, a pregnant woman in the crowd;
Guitars are strumming, scarlet dresses shimmer.
In golden gleam the chestnuts shrink and simmer;
The churches' mournful pomp looms black and proud.

The evil spirit peers from masks of white.
A square grows gloomy, hideous and stark;
Whispers arise on islands in the dark.

Lepers, who rot away perhaps at night,
Read convoluted omens of birdflight.
Siblings eye each other, trembling in the park.

Robert Firmage

De Profundis

It is a stubblefield, in which a black rain falls.
It is a brown tree, which stands there alone.
It is a hissing wind, which circles empty huts.
How sorrowful this evening.

Beyond the hamlet
Still the gentle orphan gleans her scanty grain.

Her eyes feed wide and golden in the twilight
And her womb trusts in the heavenly bridegroom.

Returning home,
The shepherds found the sweet corpse
Rotting in a thornbush.

I am a shadow far from darkened villages.
I drank
God's silence from the fountain in the grove.

Cold metal stands upon my brow;
Spiders seek my heart.
It is a light, which goes out in my mouth.

At night I found myself upon a heath,
Stiff with filth and stardust.
In the hazelbush
Crystal angels rang again.

Robert Firmage

The Rats

Into the yard the autumn moon shines white.
From the roof's edge fantastic shadows fall,
In empty windows silence dwells;
The rats then quietly steal to the surface

And dart whistling hither and thither
And a horrid vaprous breath wafts
After them out of the sewer
Through which the ghostly moonlight trembles

And they brawl, maddened with greed
And crowd the house and barns

[43]

That are filled with corn and fruit.
Icy winds grizzle in the dark.

Alexander Stillmark

Landscape

September evening: mournfully the dark cries of the
   shepherds
Ring through the dusky village; fire spits in the forge.
A black horse rears up violently; the girl's hyacinthine locks
Snatch at the ardor of its crimson nostrils.
Softly the cry of the doe freezes at the edge of the forest
And the yellow blossoms of autumn
Bend speechlessly above the blue countenance of the pond.
In red flames a tree burned down; bats flap upward with
   dark faces.

Robert Firmage

Childhood

Laden with berries the elderbush; placid the childhood
lived out in its blue hollow. The quiet branches are brooding
over the bygone path where lank, brownish grass
whips in the wind; a rustling of leaves

like blue water tumbling over rocks.
The blackbird's soft plaint. Speechless,
a shepherd follows the sun as it rolls from the autumnal
   hill.

A blue moment is nothing but soul.

A timid deer peeps out from the forest's edge, while ancient bells

and sunless hamlets merge tranquilly with the valley floor.

More pious now, you know the meaning of the dark years,

chill and autumn in lonely rooms;

and in sanctified blue, luminous footfalls echo away.

The soft rattle of an open casement; the sight of

a neglected graveyard on the hillside brings tears to the eyes.

Memories of once-told legends; but still the soul will sometimes lighten

when it recalls joyful people, burnt golden days of spring.

Michael Hofmann

Psalm II

Silence; as if the blind were sinking down by an autumn wall,

Listening with wasted brows for the flight of ravens;

Golden stillness of autumn, Father's countenance in flickering sunlight.

At evening the old village decays in the peace of brown oaks,

The red hammering of the forge, a beating heart.

Silence; in her slow hands the maid hides her hyacinth brow

Beneath fluttering sunflowers. Fear and silence

Of eyes breaking in death fills the twilit room, the wavering steps

Of the old women, the flight of the crimson mouth that slowly goes out in the gloom.

Muted evening in wine. From the low roof beams
Dropped a nocturnal moth, a nymph buried in bluish sleep.
In the yard the farmhand slaughters a lamb, the sweet smell
    of blood
Enclouds our brows, the dark coolness of the well.
The melancholy of dying asters lingers in sadness, golden
    voices in the wind.
When night comes you look upon me with mouldering
    eyes,
In blue stillness your cheeks turned to dust.

So silently a fire for weeds goes out, the black hamlet in the
    valley grows still
As if the Cross were to descend the blue hill of Calvary,
The mute earth to cast out its dead.

Alexander Stillmark

Eastern Front

The wrath of the people is dark,
Like the wild organ notes of winter storm,
The battle's crimson wave, a naked
Forest of stars.

With ravaged brows, with silver arms
To dying soldiers night comes beckoning.
In the shade of the autumn ash
Ghosts of the fallen are sighing.

Thorny wilderness girdles the town about.
From bloody doorsteps the moon
Chases terrified women.
Wild wolves have poured through the gates.

Christopher Middleton

Grodek

At evening the autumn woods resound
With deadly weapons, the golden plains
And blue lakes, the sun overhead
Rolls more darkly on; night embraces
Dying warriors, the wild lament
Of their broken mouths.
Yet silently red clouds, in which a wrathful god lives,
Gather on willow-ground
The blood that was shed, moon-coolness;
All roads flow into black decay.
Under the golden boughs of night and stars
Sister's shadow sways through the silent grove,
To greet the spirits of the heroes, the bleeding heads;
And softly the dark pipes of autumn sound in the reeds.
O prouder sorrow! You brazen altars,
The spirit's ardent flame today is fed by mighty grief,
The unborn generations.

Alexander Stillmark

Kaspar Is Dead

alas our good kaspar is dead.
who'll now hide the burning flag in the cloudpigtail and
    every day cock a black snook.
who'll now turn the coffeegrinder in the primeval tub.
who'll now lure the idyllic doe from the petrified paperbag.
who'll now blow the noses of ships parapluis windudders
    bee-fathers ozonespindles and who'll bone the pyramids.
alas alas alas our good kaspar is dead. saint dingdong
    kaspar is dead.
the grass-shark rattles his teeth heartrendingly in the
    bellbarns when his forename is spoken. therefore I shall
    go on sighing his familyname kaspar kaspar kaspar.
why hast thou forsaken us. into what form has thy great
    beautiful soul migrated. hast thou become a star or a
    chain of water hanging from a hot whirlwind or an
    udder of black light or a transparent tile on the groaning
    drum of the rocky essence.
now our tops and toes go dry and the fairies are lying
    halfcharred on the funeral pyre.
now the black skittle alley thunders behind the sun and
    nobody winds up the compasses and the pushcart wheels
    any more.
who'll now eat with the phosphorescent rat at the lonely
    barefoot table.
who'll now shoo away the siroccoco devil when he tries to
    ravish the horses.
who'll now elucidate for us the monograms in the stars.

his bust will grace the mantelpieces of all truly noble men
  but that's no consolation and snuff for a death's head.

Christopher Middleton

KURT SCHWITTERS
1887–1947

The Dadarotator

The dadarotator is intended personally for you. It is a peculiar combination of rotators, axes, and pistons, built with cadavers, nitric acid, and Merz in such a way that you enter it with complete understanding and emerge from it with none. This has great advantages for you. Invest your money in a dadarotator cure, you'll never regret it, after the treatment you'll never be able to regret anything. Rich or poor, whichever you are, it's all the same, the dadarotator frees you even from money *per se*. As a capitalist you go into the funnel, pass through several pistons, and plunge into acid. Then you come into contact with a corpse or two. Vinegar dribbles cubism dada. Then you get to see the Great Rotatory Dada. (Not the President of the Universe, as many suppose.) The dadarotator beams with wit and is pronged with about 100,000 needle-points. After you've been flung back and forth, someone will read you my latest poems, until you collapse in a faint. Then comes the fulling and dadarotating, and suddenly there you are, with a fresh haircut, out in the open, an antibourgeois. Before the treatment the eye of the needle horrifies you, after it nothing can. You'll be a rotarydada and you'll pray to the machine like someone inspired. – Amen.

Christopher Middleton

'It is autumn'

It is autumn. Swans devour the bread of their masters held together by tears. A few feeble expressionists cry out for

wine, for there's still enough wine, but no more
  Expressionism.
Long live the Kaiser, for there's no more Kaiser! Clocks clock
  the hours 25 thousand times.
I glide.
Glide noose.
Clangs a machine.
Cats hang from the wall.
A Jew is fiddling the beast on out the window.
All the way out.
It is autumn, and the swans autumn also.

Harriet Watts

Composed Picture Poem

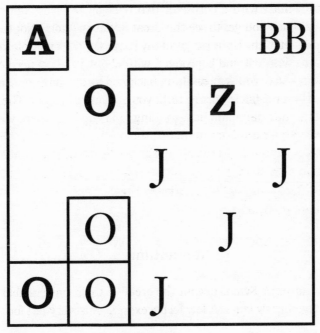

FRANZ WERFEL
1890–1945

The Fat Man in the Mirror

What's filling up the mirror? O, it is not I;
Hair-belly like a beaver's house? An old dog's eye?
    The forenoon was blue
    In the mad King's zoo
Nurse was swinging me so high, so high!

The bullies wrestled on the royal bowling green;
Hammers and sickles on their hoods of black sateen . . .
    Sulking on my swing
    The tobacco King
Sliced apples with a pen-knife for the Queen.

This *I*, who used to mouse about the parafined preserves,
And jammed a finger in the coffee-grinder, serves
    Time before the mirror.
    But this pursey terror . . .
Nurse, it is a person. *It is nerves.*

Where's the Queen-Mother waltzing like a top to
    staunch
The blood of Lewis, King of Faerie? Hip and haunch
    Lard the royal grotto;
    Straddling Lewis' motto,
Time, the Turk, its sickle on its paunch.

Nurse, Nurse, it rises on me . . . O, it starts to roll,
My apples, O, are ashes in the meerschaum bowl . . .
    If you'd only come,
    If you'd only come,
Darling, if . . . The apples that I stole,

While Nurse and I were swinging in the Old One's eye . . .
Only a fat man with his beaver on his eye,
   Only a fat man,
   Only a fat man
Bursts the mirror. O, it is not I!

Robert Lowell

NELLY SACHS
1891–1970

'O the chimneys'

And though after my skin worms destroy this body,
yet in my flesh shall I see God. – Job 19 : 26

O the chimneys
On the ingeniously devised habitations of death
When Israel's body drifted as smoke
Through the air –
Was welcomed by a star, a chimney sweep,
A star that turned black
Or was it a ray of sun?

O the chimneys!
Freedomway for Jeremiah and Job's dust –
Who devised you and laid stone upon stone
The road for refugees of smoke?

O the habitations of death,
Invitingly appointed
For the host who used to be a guest –
O you fingers
Laying the threshold
Like a knife between life and death –

O you chimneys,
O you fingers
And Israel's body as smoke through the air!

Michael Roloft

'But who emptied your shoes of sand'

But who emptied your shoes of sand
When you had to get up, to die?
The sand which Israel gathered,
Its nomad sand?
Burning Sinai sand,
Mingled with throats of nightingales,
Mingled with wings of butterflies,
Mingled with the hungry dust of serpents;
Mingled with all that fell from the wisdom of Solomon,
Mingled with what is bitter in the mystery of wormwood –

O you fingers
That emptied the deathly shoes of sand.
Tomorrow you will be dust
In the shoes of those to come.

Michael Hamburger

Chorus of the Rescued

We, the rescued,
From whose hollow bones death had begun to whittle his
    flutes,
And on whose sinews he had already stroked his bow –
Our bodies continue to lament
With their mutilated music.
We, the rescued,
The nooses wound for our necks still dangle
before us in the blue air –
Hourglasses still fill with our dripping blood.
We, the rescued,

The worms of fear still feed on us.
Our constellation is buried in dust.
We, the rescued,
Beg you:
Show us your sun, but gradually.
Lead us from star to star, step by step.
Be gentle when you teach us to live again.
Lest the song of a bird,
Or a pail being filled at the well,
Let our badly sealed pain burst forth again
and carry us away –
We beg you:
Do not show us an angry dog, not yet –
It could be, it could be
That we will dissolve into dust –
Dissolve into dust before your eyes.
For what binds our fabric together?
We whose breath vacated us,
Whose soul fled to Him out of that midnight
Long before our bodies were rescued
Into the ark of the moment.
We, the rescued,
We press your hand
We look into your eye –
But all that binds us together now is leave-taking,
The leave-taking in the dust
Binds us together with you.

   Michael Roloft

'This chain of enigmas'

This chain of enigmas
hung on the neck of night
a king's word written far away
illegible
perhaps in comet journeys
when the torn-open wound of the sky
hurts

there
within the beggar who has room
and crawling upon his knees
has measured out the roads
with his body

for the legible
must be suffered to its end
and dying learned
in patience –

Ruth and Matthew Mead

'Two hands, born to give'

Two hands, born to give,
Tore off your shoes
My beloved,
Before they killed you.
Two hands, which will have to give themselves up
When they turn to dust.
They were well tanned and dyed,
The awl had pierced them –

But who knows where a last living breath
Still dwells?
During the short parting
Between your blood and earth
They trickled sand like an hourglass
Which fills each moment with death.
Your feet!
The thoughts sped before them.
They came so quickly to God
That your feet grew weary,
Grew sore in trying to catch up with your heart.
But the calfskin
That the warm licking tongue
Of the mother-cow once stroked
Before the skin was stripped –
Was stripped once more
From your feet,
Torn off –
Oh my beloved

Ruth and Matthew Mead and Michael Hamburger

Hymn to the World

I

O whizzbang world, you luna park,
You delicious cabinet of horrors,
Watch out! Here comes Grosz,
The saddest man in Europe,
'A phenomenon of sadness.'
Hard hat pushed back,
By no means a softie!!!
A skull full of black blues,
Bright as fields of hyacinths
Or rushing express trains
Clattering over bridges –
Ragtime dancer,
Waiting with the crowds by the picket fence
For Robert E. Lee.

Horido!
By the beard of headmaster Wotan –
Afternoons of prettified sewers,
Painted over putrition,
Perfumed stench –
Grosz can sniff it.
Parbleu! I smell roast babies.

II

Get yourselves together, lads!
Crank up the Benz – 150 km

Down the ribboning roads!
You too are disgusted by the cold sweat
On your flaccid features!

Turbulence of the world!
My dear friends! Ahoy!
Greetings, y'all, boys over the water!
I.W. Hurban, Lewis, Abraham,
Theo F. Morse,
Lillian Elmore.
You converted the jungle into notes
With your New World banjo music.
Stiff standing skyscrapers.
The grey eye at liberty.
Cleanshaven and broad.

The houseboat glides down the Hudson –
With dark nights
And Negroes in black hats!

Michael Hofmann

Apfelböck, or the Lily of the Field

1
Mild was the light as Jakob Apfelböck
Struck both his father and his mother down
And shut their bodies in the linen press
And hung about the house all on his own.

2
The clouds went floating past beneath the sky
Around his house the summer winds blew mild
Inside the house he passed the time away
Who just a week before was still a child.

3
The days went by, the nights went by as well
And nothing changed except a thing or two.
Beside his parents Jakob Apfelböck
Waited to see what time would find to do.

4
The woman still delivers milk each day
Sweet thick cool skim milk, left behind the door.
What Jakob doesn't drink he pours away
For Jakob's hardly drinking any more.

5
The paper man still brings the paper round
He steps up to the house with heavy tread
And stuffs the paper in the letter box
But Jakob Apfelböck leaves it unread.

6

And when the smell of corpses filled the house
Jakob felt queasy and began to cry.
Tearfully, Jakob Apfelböck moved out
And slept henceforward on the balcony.

7

Up spoke the paper man then on his round:
What is that smell? Something gone off, I'd say.
The light was mild as Jakob Apfelböck
Said: Just some dirty clothes I shut away.

8

Up spoke the milk woman then on her round:
What is that smell? I'd say that something's died.
The light was mild as Jakob Apfelböck
Said: Just some meat that mother put aside.

9

And when they came to open the press door
Jakob stood by, the light was mild and clear
And when they asked him what he did it for
Said Jakob Apfelböck: I've no idea.

10

A few days later the milk woman said
She wondered what would happen by and by:
Would Jakob Apfelböck, the child, perhaps
Visit the grave where his poor parents lie?

John Willett

Of Swimming in Lakes and Rivers

1

In the pale summer when the winds above
Only in great trees' leaves a murmur make
You ought to lie in rivers or in ponds
As do the waterweeds which harbour pike.
The body grows light in the water. When your arm
Falls easily from water into sky
The little wind rocks it absentmindedly
Taking it likely for a brownish bough.

2

The sky at noon offers ample calm.
You close your eyes when swallows pass.
The mud is warm. Cool bubbles welling up
Show that a fish has just swum through us.
My body and thighs and resting arm
We lie in the water quite at one and still
Only when the cool fish swim through us
I sense the sun shining above the pool.

3

By the evening having grown very lazy
With lying so long, each limb begins to smart
You have to dash all that with a reckless smack
Into blue streams which scatter far apart.
It's best to last out until the evening
For then the pale shark-like sky will come
Evil and greedy over bush and river
And all things will assume their aptest form.

4

Of course you must lie upon your back
As if by habit. And drift along.
You need not swim, no, only behave as if
It's just to the mass of gravel you belong.
You should look at the sky and act
As if a woman held you, which is right.
Quite without great upheaval as the good God does
When he swims in his rivers at evening light.

Lesley Lendrum

A Cloud

One evening in the blue month of September
We lay at peace beneath an apple bough;
I took her in my arms, my gentle lover,
And held her closely like a dream come true –
While far up in the tranquil summer heaven
There was a cloud, I saw it high and clear.
It was so white and so immense above us
And, as I watched, it was no longer there.

Since then so very many different evenings
Have drifted blindly past in the general flow.
Perhaps the apple orchard has been flattened;
And if you ask me where the girl is now
I have to admit I really don't remember.
I can imagine what you're going to say
But even her face I truly can't recapture;
I only know I kissed it there that day.

Even the kiss I would have long forgotten
If that one cloud had not been up there too –

I see it and will always see it plainly,
So white and unexpected in the blue.
Perhaps the apple boughs are back in blossom,
Maybe she holds a fourth child on her knees;
The cloud, though, hung there for a moment only
And, as I watched, it broke up in the breeze.

Derek Mahon

Ballad of the Love-Death

1

Eaten away by black rain seven times over
A sordid mouth which gollops down their love
With muslin curtains damp as shrouds for cover:
Such is the attic which they'll never leave.

2

Leprous the wallpaper, mildewed and crumbling!
Shut in by wooden boards they're welded, tight:
To this white couple in its heavenly coupling
The threadbare heaven seems a sheer delight.

3

To start with he'll sit there in damp towels, chewing
The black cheroots she gives him. Mouth askew
He'll kill the time nodding his head, and cooing
With drooping eyelid that he loves her true.

4

Such hairiness, she feels, and oh, such wisdom!
He sees the day dissolve, his eyes a slot
While, green as soap, the clouds shut off the sky's dome
And all he thinks is: how my shirt will rot.

[65]

5

They're pouring brandy down their dried-up bodies
He's feeding her on evening's pale green light
And now her things are covered with red blotches
And now her face is slowly going white.

6

She's like some waterlogged field by the river
(They're deaf, they're orphaned, all their flesh is drained!)
He wants his sleep, but will she let him leave her?
Green sky above, that recently has rained!

7

The second day they used the sweat-stained curtains
As stiffened sheets to wrap their corpses in
And packed their thighs with greasy strips of shirting
Because they've learned that's where the chills begin.

8

And, oh, love stabbed them through and through, so neatly
As when God's hailstones through the water hiss.
And deep within them, gutting them completely
And thick as yeast, welled up green bitterness.

9

Their hair filled with the smells of sweat and urine
They'll never see again the break of day.
Yet, years from now, the day will come and pour in
To that wallpaper vault, bestial and grey.

10

Oh, her young pearly body, soft as butter!
Beaten so raw by wood and love right through
Dissolves like wood in some old battered cutter
Beneath a storm. Like grass soggy with dew.

11

Oh, but the hand that holds her breast is grassy!
And black the stench of plague in every limb!
Mild air rinsed down the window, hard and glassy
While still the rotten cupboard sheltered them.

12

Like dishwater the evening rinsed the skylight
Its curtains mangy with tobacco smoke.
Across green seas two lovers in the twilight
Drift, soaked in love, like some rain-sodden hulk

13

Which, breaking up deep in the tropic oceans
Hangs there between seaweed and the pallid fish
And, far below, starts gentle rocking motions
Caught from the surface where the salt winds swish.

14

On the fourth morning neighbours got up, fetched their
Thundering sledgehammers and smashed down the door
They heard the silence, saw the corpses stretched there
(And murmured saying what a greenish glare

15

Can come from faces); what is more, the bed kept
Its smell of love, the window burst with frost:
A corpse is such a cold thing! And a thread crept
Thin, cold and black, towards them from its breast.

John Willett

Of Poor B.B.

1

I, Bertolt Brecht, came out of the black forests.
My mother moved me into the cities as I lay
Inside her body. And the coldness of the forests
Will be inside me till my dying day.

2

In the asphalt city I'm at home. From the very start
Provided with every last sacrament:
With newspapers. And tobacco. And brandy
To the end mistrustful, lazy and content.

3

I'm polite and friendly to people. I put on
A hard hat because that's what they do.
I say: they are animals with a quite peculiar smell
And I say: does it matter? I am too.

4

Before noon on my empty rocking chairs
I'll sit a woman or two, and with an untroubled eye
Look at them steadily and say to them:
Here you have someone on whom you can't rely.

5

Towards evening it's men that I gather round me
And then we address one another as 'gentlemen'.
They're resting their feet on my table tops
And say: things will get better for us. And I don't ask when.

6

In the grey light before morning the pine trees piss
And their vermin, the birds, raise their twitter and cheep.

At that hour in the city I drain my glass, then throw
The cigar butt away and worriedly go to sleep.

7
We have sat, an easy generation
In houses held to be indestructible
(Thus we built those tall boxes on the island of Manhattan
And those thin aerials that amuse the Atlantic swell).

8
Of those cities will remain what passed through them, the
     wind!
The house makes glad the eater: he clears it out.
We know that we're only tenants, provisional ones
And after us there will come: nothing worth talking about.

9
In the earthquakes to come, I very much hope
I shall keep my cigar alight, embittered or no
I, Bertolt Brecht, carried off to the asphalt cities
From the black forests inside my mother long ago.

Michael Hamburger

Thoughts on The Duration of Exile

I

Don't knock any nails in the wall
Just throw your coat on the chair.
Why plan for four days?
Tomorrow you'll go back home.

Leave the little tree without water.
Why plant a tree now?

You'll pack your bags and be away
Before it's as high as a doorstep.

Pull your cap over your eyes when people pass.
What use thumbing through a foreign grammar?
The message that calls you home
Is written in a language you know.

As whitewash peels from the ceiling
(Do nothing to stop it!)
So the block of force will crumble
That has been set up at the frontier
To keep out justice.

II

Look at the nail you knocked into the wall:
When do you think you will go back?
Do you want to know what your heart of hearts is saying?
Day after day
You work for the liberation.
You sit in your room, writing.
Do you want to know what you think of your work?
Look at the little chestnut tree in the corner of the yard –
You carried a full can of water to it.

Christopher Middleton

Place of Refuge

An oar lies on the roof. A moderate wind
Will not carry away the thatch.
In the yard posts are set for
The children's swing.

The mail comes twice a day
Where letters would be welcome.
Down the Sound come the ferries.
The house has four doors to escape by.

John Willett

To Those Born Later

I

Truly, I live in dark times!
The guileless word is folly. A smooth forehead
Suggests insensitivity. The man who laughs
Has simply not yet had
The terrible news.

What kind of times are they, when
A talk about trees is almost a crime
Because it implies silence about so many horrors?
That man there calmly crossing the street
Is already perhaps beyond the reach of his friends
Who are in need?

It is true I still earn my keep
But, believe me, that is only an accident. Nothing
I do gives me the right to eat my fill.
By chance I've been spared. (If my luck breaks, I am lost.)

They say to me: Eat and drink! Be glad you have it!
But how can I eat and drink if I snatch what I eat
From the starving, and
My glass of water belongs to one dying of thirst?
And yet I eat and drink.

I would also like to be wise.
In the old books it says what wisdom is:
To shun the strife of the world and to live out
Your brief time without fear
Also to get along without violence
To return good for evil
Not to fulfil your desires but to forget them
Is accounted wise.
All this I cannot do:
Truly, I live in dark times.

II

I came to the cities in a time of disorder
When hunger reigned there.
I came among men in a time of revolt
And I rebelled with them.
So passed my time
Which had been given to me on earth.

My food I ate between battles
To sleep I lay down among murderers
Love I practised carelessly
And nature I looked at without patience.
So passed my time
Which had been given to me on earth.

All roads led into the mire in my time.
My tongue betrayed me to the butchers.
There was little I could do. But those in power
Sat safer without me: that was my hope.
So passed my time
Which had been given to me on earth.

Our forces were slight. Our goal
Lay far in the distance
It was clearly visible, though I myself
Was unlikely to reach it.
So passed my time
Which had been given to me on earth.

III

You who will emerge from the flood
In which we have gone under
Remember
When you speak of our failings
The dark time too
Which you have escaped.

For we went, changing countries oftener than our shoes
Through the wars of the classes, despairing
When there was injustice only, and no rebellion.

And yet we know:
Hatred, even of meanness
Contorts the features.
Anger, even against injustice
Makes the voice hoarse. Oh, we
Who wanted to prepare the ground for friendliness
Could not ourselves be friendly.

But you, when the time comes at last
And man is a helper to man
Think of us
With forbearance.

John Willett

Motto

This, then, is all. It's not enough, I know.
At least I'm still alive, as you may see.
I'm like the man who took a brick to show
How beautiful his house used once to be.

John Willett

1940

I

Spring is coming. The gentle winds
Are freeing the cliffs of their winter ice.
Trembling, the peoples of the north await
The battle fleets of the house-painter.

II

Out of the libraries
Emerge the butchers.
Pressing their children closer
Mothers stand and humbly search
The skies for the inventions of learned men.

III

The designers sit
Hunched in the drawing offices:
One wrong figure, and the enemy's cities
Will remain undestroyed.

IV

Fog envelops
The road
The poplars
The farms and
The artillery.

V

I am now living on the small island of Lidingö.
But one night recently
I had heavy dreams and I dreamed I was in a city
And discovered that its street signs
Were in German. I awoke
Bathed in sweat, saw the fir tree
Black as night before my window, and realised with relief:
I was in a foreign land.

VI

My young son asks me: Should I learn mathematics?
What for, I'm inclined to say. That two bits of bread are
    more than one
You'll notice anyway.
My young son asks me: Should I learn French?
What for, I'm inclined to say. That empire is going under.
Just rub your hand across your belly and groan
And you'll be understood all right.
My young son asks me: Should I learn history?
What for, I'm inclined to say. Learn to stick your head in the
    ground
Then maybe you'll come through.

Yes, learn mathematics, I tell him
Learn French, learn history!

VII

In front of the whitewashed wall
Stands the black military case with the manuscripts.
On it lie the smoking things with the copper ashtrays.
The Chinese scroll depicting the Doubter
Hangs above it. The masks are there too. And by the
    bedstead
Stands the little six-valve radio.
Mornings
I turn it on and hear
The victory bulletins of my enemies.

VIII

Fleeing from my fellow-countrymen
I have now reached Finland. Friends
Whom yesterday I didn't know, put up some beds
In clean rooms. Over the radio
I hear the victory bulletins of the scum of the earth.
    Curiously
I examine a map of the continent. High up in Lapland
Towards the Arctic Ocean
I can still see a small door.

Sammy McLean

On Thinking about Hell

On thinking about Hell, I gather
My brother Shelley found it was a place

[76]

Much like the city of London. I
Who live in Los Angeles and not in London
Find, on thinking about Hell, that it must be
Still more like Los Angeles.

In Hell too
There are, I've no doubt, these luxuriant gardens
With flowers as big as trees, which of course wither
Unhesitantly if not nourished with very expensive water.
    And fruit markets
With great heaps of fruit, albeit having
Neither smell nor taste. And endless processions of cars
Lighter than their own shadows, faster than
Mad thoughts, gleaming vehicles in which
Jolly-looking people come from nowhere and are nowhere
    bound.
And houses, built for happy people, therefore standing
    empty
Even when lived in.

The houses in Hell, too, are not all ugly.
But the fear of being thrown on the street
Wears down the inhabitants of the villas no less than
The inhabitants of the shanty towns.

Nicholas Jacobs

Hollywood Elegies

I

The village of Hollywood was planned according to the
    notion
People in these parts have of heaven. In these parts
They have come to the conclusion that God

Requiring a heaven and a hell, didn't need to
Plan two establishments but
Just the one: heaven. It
Serves the unprosperous, unsuccessful
As hell.

II

By the sea stand the oil derricks. Up the canyons
The gold prospectors' bones lie bleaching. Their sons
Built the dream factories of Hollywood.
The four cities
Are filled with the oily smell
Of films.

III

The city is named after the angels
And you meet angels on every hand.
They smell of oil and wear golden pessaries
And, with blue rings round their eyes
Feed the writers in their swimming pools every morning.

IV

Beneath the green pepper trees
The musicians play the whore, two by two
With the writers. Bach
Has written a Strumpet Voluntary. Dante wriggles
His shrivelled bottom.

V

The angels of Los Angeles
Are tired out with smiling. Desperately

Behind the fruit stalls of an evening
They buy little bottles
Containing sex odours.

VI

Above the four cities the fighter planes
Of the Defense Department circle at a great height
So that the stink of greed and poverty
Shall not reach them.

John Willett

Of Sprinkling the Garden

O sprinkling the garden, to enliven the green!
Watering the thirsty trees. Give them more than enough
And do not forget the shrubs
Even those without berries, the exhausted
Niggardly ones. And do not neglect
The weeds growing between the flowers, they too
Are thirsty. Nor water only
The fresh grass or only the scorched.
Even the naked soil you must refresh.

Patrick Bridgwater

from Buckow Elegies

CHANGING THE WHEEL

I sit by the roadside
The driver changes the wheel.
I do not like the place I have come from.

I do not like the place I am going to.
Why with impatience do I
Watch him changing the wheel?

Michael Hamburger

THE SOLUTION

After the uprising of the 17th June
The Secretary of the Writers' Union
Had leaflets distributed in the Stalinallee
Stating that the people
Had forfeited the confidence of the government
And could win it back only
By redoubled efforts. Would it not be easier
In that case for the government
To dissolve the people
And elect another?

Derek Bowman

EIGHT YEARS AGO

There was a time
When all was different here.
The butcher's wife knows.
The postman has too erect a gait.
And what was the electrician?

Derek Bowman

READING A LATE GREEK POET

At the time when their fall was certain –
On the ramparts the lament for the dead had begun –
The Trojans adjusted small pieces, small pieces

[80]

In the triple wooden gates, small pieces.
And began to take courage, to hope.

The Trojans too, then.

Michael Hamburger

'AND I ALWAYS THOUGHT'

And I always thought: the very simplest words
Must be enough. When I say what things are like
Everyone's heart must be torn to shreds.
That you'll go down if you don't stand up for yourself.
Surely you see that.

Michael Hamburger

PETER HUCHEL
1903–1981

Landscape Beyond Warsaw

March with its sharp pick
Splits the ice of the sky.
From the cracks light pours
Billowing down
On to telegraph wires and bare main roads.
At noon white it roosts in the reeds,
A great bird.
When it spreads its claws, brightly
The webs gleam out of thin mist.

Nightfall is brief.
Then more shallow than a dog's palate
The sky arches.
A hill smokes
As though still the huntsmen
Were sitting there by the damp winter fire.
Where have they gone?
The hare's tracks in the snow
Once told us where.

Michael Hamburger

Roads

Choked sunset glow
Of crashing time.
Roads. Roads.
Intersections of flight.
Cart tracks across the ploughed field
That with the eyes
Of killed horses
Saw the sky in flames.

Nights with lungs full of smoke,
With the hard breath of the fleeing
When shots
Struck the dusk.
Out of a broken gate
Ash and wind came without a sound,
A fire
That sullenly chewed the darkness.

Corpses,
Flung over the rail tracks,
Their stifled cry
Like a stone on the palate.
A black
Humming cloth of flies
Closed their wounds.

Michael Hamburger

The Poplars

Time with your rusty scythe,
Late you went on your way,
Up the narrow path
And past the two poplars.
They swam
In the sky's thin water.
A white stone drowned.
Was it the moon, desolation's eye?

Dusk on the graveside bushes.
It wound its cloth
Coarsely woven of grass and mist
Around helmets and bones.
The dawn light, encrusted with ice,
Threw glinting shards into rushes.
In silence the fisherman pushed
His boat into the river. The water's
Freezing voice complained,
Bearing corpse after corpse downstream.

But who buried them in the frosty clay,
In ashes and mud,
Disaster's old footprints?
Amid the razing impact of war
The ploughed field glistens, the corn blade's power wells
    up.
And where the paring plough turns,
Where stubble falls,
On the slope the two poplars remain.
They loom into light
As the antennae of Earth.

Lovely our homeland is
When over the green brass disc
Of the pond a crane cries
And gold gathers
In October's blue vault;
When corn and milk sleep in the store-room
The sparks fly up
From night's anvil.
The world's sooty forge
Begins to fan its fire.
It beats out
The glowing iron of dawn.
And ash falls
On the shadows of bats.

Michael Hamburger

The Garden of Theophrastus

When at noon the white fire of verses
Flickering dances above the urns,
Remember, my son. Remember the vanished
Who planted their conversations like trees.
The garden is dead, more heavy my breathing,
Preserve the hour, here Theophrastus walked,
With oak bark to feed the soil and enrich it,
To bandage with fiber the wounded bole.
And olive tree splits the brickwork grown brittle
And still is a voice in the mote-laden heat.
Their order was to fell and uproot it,
Your light is fading, defenceless leaves.

Michael Hamburger

Psalm

That from the seed of men
No man
And from the seed of the olive tree
No olive tree
Shall grow,
This you must measure
With the yardstick of death.

Those who live
Under the earth
In a capsule of cement,
Their strength is like
A blade of grass
Lashed by snow in a blizzard.

The desert now will be history.
Termites with their pincers
Write it
On sand.

And no one will enquire
Into a species
Eagerly bent
On self-extinction.

Michael Hamburger

The Mudcatchers

One night from a hole in the asphalt
naked men arrived.
They smelled of soapy mud.
In his net
one of them carried
dead fish
and green water rats.
Effluent oozed from their boots.
No one wanted to see them
in the town,
everyone locked his door.
They crossed the market square and vanished
in the shrubs of the small allotments.
A glittering mussel shell
clung to the hair of one.
For a long time it glimmered
in the street's oily mirror.

Michael Hamburger

GÜNTER EICH
1907–1972

Inventory

This is my cap,
this is my coat,
here is my shaving set
in a linen bag.

A tin can:
my plate, my cup,
in the metal
I have scratched my name.

Scratched it with this
precious nail,
which I hide
from greedy eyes.

In my haversack are
a pair of woolen socks
and some things I don't
tell anyone about,

it serves as a pillow
at night for my head.
The cardboard lies here
between me and the earth.

The pencil lead
I love the most:
by day it writes verses for me
that I have thought up by night.

This is my notebook,
this is my canvas,
this is my towel,
this is my thread.

Charlotte Melin

Report from a Spa

I haven't tried the water yet,
that can wait.
But the redecorated station
implies future,
which makes me mulish.

Corpuscle count and forest ozone,
suspicion of the spa doctors.
Nature
is a form of negation.
Better to stick to
the ditties in the spa newsletter.

Michael Hofmann

Brothers Grimm

Nettlebush.
The burnt children
Wait behind the cellar windows.
Their parents have gone out,
saying they will be back soon.

First came the wolf,
bringing rolls,

[89]

the hyena wanted to borrow a garden-fork,
the scorpion came for the TV guide.

Without flames
the nettlebush burns outside.
Their parents
are gone a long time.

Michael Hofmann

Perspective from the Spezial-Keller

A backdrop for my bibulousness
and smoke towards Julia's sketches,
no fortune
to make me attractive to anyone,
and my friends
have yet to show.

Michael Hofmann

Tips from the Posthumous Papers

Asked after the lime-kiln:
pole-cats live there
and kindly girls.

To the scrapheap
the onset of cataracts,
creation right up against
my reading-glasses.

I don't hear much:
gear changes,
screams for help in silence.

[90]

I have always loved nettles,
and only now learned
of their usefulness.

Michael Hofmann

Confined to Bed

Angina days, blue snow,
time tucked away
in cut-out arches,
time is blue, time is snow,
red sleeves, black hat,
time is a yellow woman.

Angina days, Swiss,
blue Devon,
black Cambrium,
commedia dell'arte time,
slipper red and Silurian red,
wall map of England yellow and time.

Angina days, blue Kent,
time so yellow that none
can tell it, a black index finger
protrudes from a blue glove
and points you the way home
along the red wall.

Michael Hofmann

ERNST MEISTER

1911–1979

Human Monologue

We are used to the world.
We love the world as we love ourselves.
Were the world suddenly changed
We would weep.

In nothingness questions dwell.
In nothingness the pupils are large.
If there was no nothingness
We would not sleep now
and the coming dream
would sink among giant bashful stones.

Georg M. Gugelberger

JOHANNES BOBROWSKI
1917–1965

Childhood

Then I loved
the oriole –
the toll of bells sounded
above, sank low
through the greenwood,

when we squatted at the edge of the wood,
threaded red berries
on a grass-blade; the grey Jew
went by
with his cart.

At noon then the beasts stood
in the alders' black shadows
flicking away the flies
with angry tails.

Then the streaming rain-flood
fell from the open
sky; after all that darkness
the drops tasted
like earth.

Or the lads came
along the towpath with the horses,
on the shining brown
backs they rode laughing
across the deep.

Behind the fence
hummed clouds of bees.

Later the silver rattle of fear
ran through the thorn thicket
by the reedy lake.
It grew wild, a hedge,
darkening window and door.

Then the old woman sang in her
fragrant chamber. The lamp
hummed. The men
entered calling over their shoulders
to the dogs.

Night, long interlocked with silence –
time, slipping away, bitterer,
lasting from verse to verse:
childhood –
then I loved the oriole.

Ruth and Matthew Mead

Latvian Songs

My father the hawk.
Grandfather the wolf.
And my forefather the rapacious fish in the sea.

I, unbearded, a fool,
lurching against the fences,
my black hands strangling a lamb
in the early light. I,

who beat the animals
instead of the white
master, I follow the rattling caravans
on washed-out roads,

I pass through the glances
of the gipsy women. Then
on the Baltic shore I meet Uexküll, the master.
He walks beneath the moon.

Behind him, the darkness speaks.

Ruth and Matthew Mead

Unsaid

Heavy,
I grow down,
I spread roots
in the ground,
the waters of earth
find me, rise,
I taste bitterness – you
are without earth,
a bird of the air, lighter
always in light,
only my fear still
holds you
in the earthly wind.

Ruth and Matthew Mead

Report

Bajla Gelblung,
escaped in Warsaw
from a transport from the Ghetto,
the girl took to the woods,
armed, was picked up

[95]

as partisan
in Brest-Litovsk,
wore a military coat (Polish),
was interrogated by German
officers, there is
a photo, the officers are young
chaps, faultlessly uniformed,
with faultless faces,
their bearing
is unexceptionable.

Ruth and Matthew Mead

Mozart

The buckle is loose
on my shoe, there was
a silver button there,
my throat hurts me, my eyes,
if I closed them –

Then I noticed
the new wrinkle
in Colloredo's face . . .
the little house in Prague
floating down the slope,
bushes, a white wave,
in front of it – when the endless
rain was over, the light
one evening
on Stein's piano.

There was still a music
to be written,

wood, a thudding, earthly,
beneath the feet, a door
bangs in the house, I do not question,
I alone hear it,
I do not like it when Constanze
laughs
with her glassy mouth.

Ruth and Matthew Mead

Trakl

Brow.
The brown beam.
Floorboards. The steps
to the window.
The green of large leaves. Signs,
written over the table.

The splintering threshold. And
deserted. Slowly
pursuing the stranger
under the jackdaws' wings
in grass and dust
the road with no name.

Michael Hamburger

RAINER BRAMBACH
1917–83

Morning

Each day the milkman comes at six
A little after seven the newspaper lady limps along
At eight I start coming round
On the table there's still the wine bottle
from last night and the glass, empty.
And there too are the letters
all of them sincerely mine –
Get up, walk around, read
Ecclesiastes eleven
truly the light is sweet
and a pleasant thing it is for the eyes to behold the sun . . .

Michael Hofmann

Single Men

One collects stones.
One acquires stamps.
A third plays chess by mail
and one stands and lurks in the park in the evenings.
One studies Russian.
One reads Shakespeare.
One writes one letter after another,
and one drinks wine in the evening,
otherwise nothing to report.
They drink, read, lurk, acquire,
these men alone in their evening.
They write, study, play, collect,

each for himself after the close of work.
One visits the operetta.
One listens to Bach.
One keeps a secret.
Like a dog on a chain,
he runs down the avenues, night after night.

Michael Hofmann

Memory of France

Together with me recall: the sky of Paris, that giant autumn
  crocus . . .
We went shopping for hearts at the flower girl's booth:
they were blue and they opened up in the water.
It began to rain in our room,
and our neighbour came in, Monsieur Le Songe, a lean little
  man.
We played cards, I lost the irises of my eyes;
you lent me your hair, I lost it, he struck us down.
He left by the door, the rain followed him out.
We were dead and were able to breathe.

Michael Hamburger

Corona

Autumn eats its leaf out of my hand: we are friends.
From the nuts we shell time and we teach it to walk:
then time returns to the shell.

In the mirror it's Sunday,
in dream there is room for sleeping,
our mouths speak the truth.

My eye moves down to the sex of my loved one:
we look at each other,
we exchange dark words,
we love each other like poppy and recollection,
we sleep like wine in the conches,
like the sea in the moon's blood ray.

We stand by the window embracing, and people look up
    from the street:
it is time they knew!
It is time the stone made an effort to flower,
time unrest had a beating heart.
It is time it were time.

It is time.

    Michael Hamburger

Deathfugue

Black milk of daybreak we drink it at evening
we drink it at midday and morning we drink it at night
we drink and we drink
we shovel a grave in the air where you won't lie too
    cramped
A man lives in the house he plays with his vipers he writes
he writes when it grows dark to Deutschland your golden
    hair Margareta
he writes it and steps out of doors and the stars are all
    sparkling he whistles his hounds to stay close
he whistles his Jews into rows has them shovel a grave in
    the ground
he commands us play up for the dance

Black milk of daybreak we drink you at night
we drink you at morning and midday we drink you at
    evening
we drink and we drink
A man lives in the house he plays with his vipers he writes
he writes when it grows dark to Deutschland your golden
    hair Margareta

Your ashen hair Shulamith we shovel a grave in the air
      where you won't lie too cramped

He shouts dig this earth deeper you lot there you others sing
      up and play
he grabs for the rod in his belt he swings it his eyes are so
      blue
stick your spades deeper you lot there you others play on for
      the dancing

Black milk of daybreak we drink you at night
we drink you at midday and morning we drink you at
      evening
we drink and we drink
a man lives in the house your goldenes Haar Margareta
your aschenes Haar Shulamith he plays with his vipers

He shouts play death more sweetly this Death is a master
      from Deutschland
he shouts scrape your strings darker you'll rise up as smoke
      to the sky
you'll then have a grave in the clouds where you won't lie
      too cramped

Black milk of daybreak we drink you at night
we drink you at midday Death is a master aus
      Deutschland
we drink you at evening and morning we drink and we
      drink
this Death is ein Meister aus Deutschland his eye it is
      blue
he shoots you with shot made of lead shoots you level and
      true
a man lives in the house your goldenes Haar Margarete

he looses his hounds on us grants us a grave in the air
he plays with his vipers and daydreams der Tod ist ein
    Meister aus Deutschland

dein goldenes Haar Margarete
dein aschenes Haar Sulamith

   John Felstiner

'Count the almonds'

Count the almonds,
count what was bitter and kept you awake,
count me in:

I looked for your eye when you opened it, no one was
    looking at you,
I spun that secret thread
on which the dew you were thinking
slid down to the jugs
guarded by words that to no one's heart found their way.

Only there did you wholly enter the name that is yours,
sure-footed stepped into yourself,
freely the hammers swung in the bell frame of your silence,
the listened for reached you,
what is dead put its arm round you also
and the three of you walked through the evening.

Make me bitter.
Count me among the almonds.

   Michael Hamburger

Tenebrae

Near are we, Lord,
near and graspable.

Grasped already, Lord,
clawed into each other, as if
each of our bodies were
your body, Lord.

Pray, Lord,
pray to us,
we are near.

Wind-skewed we went there,
went there to bend
over pit and crater.

Went to the water-trough, Lord.

It was blood, it was
what you shed, Lord.

It shined.

It cast your image into our eyes, Lord.
Eyes and mouth stand so open and void, Lord.
We have drunk, Lord.
The blood and the image that was in the blood, Lord.

Pray, Lord.
We are near.

John Felstiner

Matière de Bretagne

Gorselight, yellow, the slopes
suppurate heavenward, the thorn
woos the wound, bells ring
within, it is evening, Nothing
rolls its seas to the service,
the blood sail makes for you.

Dry, the bed behind you
fills with silt, its hour
clogs with rushes, above,
by the star, the milky
tideways jabber through mud, date shell,
below, bunched, yawns into blueness, a shrub
of transience, beautiful,
meets your memory, greets it.

(Did you know me,
hands? I went
the forked way you showed me, my mouth
spewed out its chippings, I went, my time,
a shifting snow-wall, cast its shadow – did you know
    me?)

Hands, the thorn-
wooed wound, hands,
Nothing is ringing its seas.
Hands, in the gorselight, the
blood sail
makes for you.

You
you teach
you teach your hands
you teach your hands you teach
you teach your hands
                how to sleep

Michael Hamburger

'There was earth inside them'

There was earth inside them, and
they dug.

They dug and dug, and so
their day went past, their night. And they did not praise
    God,
who, so they heard, wanted all this,
who, so they heard, witnessed all this.

They dug and heard nothing more;
they did not grow wise, invented no song,
devised for themselves no sort of language.
They dug.

There came a stillness then, came also storm,
all of the oceans came.
I dig, you dig, and it digs too, the worm,
and the singing there says: They dig.

O one, o none, o no one, o you:
Where did it go then, making for nowhere?
O you dig and I dig, and I dig through to you,
and the ring on our finger awakens.

John Felstiner

Tübingen, January

Eyes talked in-
to blindness.
Their – 'a
riddle, what is purely
arisen' –, their
memory of
floating Hölderlintowers, gullenswirled.

Visits of drowned joiners to
these
plunging words:

Came, if there
came a man,
came a man to the world, today, with
the patriarchs'
light-beard: he could,
if he spoke of this
time, he
could
only babble and babble,
ever- ever-
moremore.

('Pallaksch. Pallaksch.')

John Felstiner

'Temple-pincers'

Temple-pincers
eyed by your cheekbone.
Their silver gleam
where they bit in:
you and the rest of your sleep –
soon
it's your birthday.

John Felstiner

'Don't write yourself'

Don't write yourself
in between worlds,
rise up against
multiple meanings,

trust the trail of tears
and learn to live.

John Felstiner

FRIEDERIKE MAYRÖCKER

1924–

Ostia Will Receive You

I'll be in Ostia
I'll be there waiting for you
I'll be there embracing you
I shall be holding your hands in Ostia
I'll be there
in Ostia
there's the mouth of the Tiber
that age-old river

I shall not be in Ostia
I shall not be there waiting for you
I shall not be there embracing you
I shan't be holding your hands in Ostia
I shall not be there
in Ostia
there's the mouth of that age-old river
the Tiber

Reinhold Grimm

Lost and Near

Don't know why but
suddenly between
Lastenstrasse and the Ring the feeling
came over me again I'd like
once more to see you
Someone
walking toward me looked

like you, I sought
more signs, the white and blue quilt,
the sharp
crusts in ice, a flash
came from a photo automat, the moon
went dimmer, shifted
into the zenith, jackdaws
crisscrossed and called, there was a smell
of baked apples, in my head
something swam, my
eyes were hot, in the illuminated top
angle of the wall your
limbs in a tangle of ivy,
and stretching up and up
your blackened hand . . .

Christopher Middleton

from the big e

e) even sex-hexed men mend nets
   even zen-spent men need mend
   even elf-seen men bend necks
   even sex-flecked men's seeds fend
   even zen-helped men breed sex seeds
   even elf-helped men tend wrecks
   even sex-hexed men mend nets

e) errers err re errers
   e'en ere errers err errers erst err'd
   e'en ere errers stretch erect extended
   fete genteel genes effete
   vexed errers better stet bedwetters err'r
   lest vexed errers kept stetted ere bedwetters get better

e) ever seek ether
   needles even seek ether-seekers
   needles even seek ether needle-seekers seek
   ether evens eden
   ether evens needle-eden
   ether needles ethers even eden-needles seek
   ether greets lechers
   lechers enter
   lechers enter needles even
   lechers enter needle-ether
   lechers enter eden

e) sweet herbs sweeten sweeter elements
   wet stems whet nettles' wetter welt
   tethers tethered tetherers' tenderer elements

effected stretches reflect defect tenements
quellers squelch quellers' nerve-swell
sellers sell cells' nerve-swelled whey
hell's belt held helen's element
feller's press'd-festered neck festers best

Guy Bennett

marking a turn

1944	*1945*
war	war
war	war
war	war
war	war
war	may
war	
war	
war	
war	
war	
war	
war	

Rosmarie Waldrop

oberflächenübersetzung

mai hart lieb zapfen eibe hold
er renn bohr in sees kai
so was sieht wenn mai lauft begehen
so es seiht nahe emma mahen
so biet wenn arschel grollt
ohr leck mit ei!
seht steil dies fader rosse mahen
in teig kurt wisch mai desto bier
baum deutsche deutsch bajonett schur alp eiertier

(surface translation – after William Wordsworth)

my heart leaps up when I behold
a rainbow in the sky
so was it when my life began
so it is now I am a man
so be it when I shall grow old
or let me die!
the child is father of the man
and I could wish my days to be
each bound to each by natural piety

[may hard dear cone yew fair
he run drill in lake's quay
so something sees when may runs walk
so it sees near emma mow
so offer when little arse scolds
ear lick with egg!
see steep this dull horses mow
in dough kurt wipe may the more beer
tree german german bayonet stir alp ballbeast]

   E.J.

[113]

HEINZ PIONTEK
1925–2003

Circa 1800

The natives'
shy heel-click

while some blueblood
clumps around.

Lines of verse.
Blows with a stick.

Many have a dream
of being sold.

Wet ink glistens.

Classicism
in Germany.

Michael Hofmann

INGE MÜLLER
1925–1966

Under the Rubble III

When I went to fetch water
The house collapsed on top of me
We supported the house
The abandoned dog and me.
Don't ask me how we did it
I don't remember.
Ask the dog.

Michael Hofmann

The Black Cart

Here comes the black cart
The horse walks at a trot
And whoever can't keep up
Gets to go in the black cart.

Michael Hofmann

'You promised you would walk with me'

You promised you would walk with me
In the sun
And by the river, where the trees
Are still in leaf
. . .
The trees have been in leaf
Four times since then

Days off are as rare
As sun in late fall –
Leaves rustle
On our desks.

Michael Hofmann

'I left you last night'

I left you last night
For a long time – I have a feeling, for good.
The morning was a grey room
And when you went out the streets were full of smoke.

Michael Hofmann

INGEBORG BACHMANN
1926–1973

The Time Allotted

Worse days are coming.
The time allotted for disavowals
Comes due on the skyline.
Soon you will lace up your shoes
And drive the dogs back to the marshes.

For the intestines of fish
Have frozen up in the wind.
The lupines burn with a feeble light.
Your glance cuts through the fog:
The time allotted for disavowals
Comes due on the skyline.

In the distance your mistress sinks under the sand,
It pours through her wind-loosened hair,
It covers her words,
It turns her to silence,
It finds her mortal
And ready to part
With every embrace.

Don't look around.
Lace up your shoes.
Drive the dogs back.
Throw the fish in the sea.
Smother the lupines!

Worse days are coming.

Jerome Rothenberg

Departure from England

I have barely stepped upon your land,
silent country, barely disturbed a stone.
I was lifted so high by your sky,
placed so in clouds, mist, and remoteness,
that I had already left you
the moment I set anchor.

You have closed my eyes
with sea breeze and oak leaf,
upon the tears I cried
you let the grasses feed;
out of my dreams, suns dared
to venture across the land,
yet everything disappeared
as soon as your day began.
Everything remained unspoken.

Through streets flapped the great, gray birds
that singled me out for expulsion.
Was I ever here?

I didn't want to be seen.

My eyes are open.
Sea breeze and oak leaf?
Under the serpentine sea
in place of you I see
the country of my soul succumb.

I have never stepped on its land.

Peter Filkins

Autumn Maneuver

I don't say: ah, yesterday. With worthless
summer money pocketed, we lie again
on the chaff of scorn, in time's autumn maneuver.
And the escape southward isn't feasible for us
as it is for the birds. In the evening
trawlers and gondolas pass, and sometimes
a splinter of dream-filled marble pierces me
in the eye, where I am most vulnerable to beauty.

In the papers I read about the cold
and its effects, about fools and dead men,
about exiles, murderers and myriads
of ice floes, but little that comforts me.
Why should it be otherwise? In the face of the beggar
who comes at noon I slam the door, for we live in peacetime
and one can spare oneself such a sight, but not
the joyless dying of leaves in the rain.

Let's take a trip! Let us stroll under cypresses
or even under palms or in the orange groves
to see at reduced rates sunsets
that are beyond compare! Let us forget
the unanswered letters to yesterday!
Time works wonders. But if it arrives inconveniently
with the knocking of guilt: we're not at home.
In the heart's cellar, sleepless, I find myself again
on the chaff of scorn, in time's autumn maneuver.

Peter Filkins

Salt and Bread

Now the wind sends its rails ahead;
we will follow in slow trains
and inhabit these islands,
intimacy exchanged for intimacy.

Into the hand of my oldest friend
I place the key to my post; the rain man will now manage
my darkened house and complete
the lines of the ledger which I drew up
after I was seldom around.

You, in fever-white vestments,
gather the exiled and tear
from the flesh of cactus, a thorn
– symbol of impotence
to which we meekly bow.

We know
that we'll remain the continent's captives,
and again we'll succumb to its troubled ills,
and the tides of truth
will be no rarer.

For sleeping in the cliff
is the barely lit skull,
the claw hangs in the claw
in the dark stone, and the stigmata
are healed in the violet of the volcano.

Of the great storms of light,
none has come to life.

So I gather the salt
when the sea overcomes us,

and turn back
and lay it on the threshold
and step into the house.

We share bread with the rain;
bread, a debt, and a house.

Peter Filkins

Days in White

These days I rise with the birches
and brush the corn hair from my brow
before a mirror of ice.

Blended with my breath,
milk is beaten.
This early it foams easily.
And where I fog the pane there appears,
traced by a child-like finger,
again your name: Innocence!
After all these years.

These days I feel no pain
that I can forget
or that I must remember.

I love. Incandescently
I love and give thanks with Ave Marias.
I learned them with ease.

These days I think of the albatross
with whom I swung
up and over
into an uncharted land.

On the horizon I ascertain,
splendid in the sunset,
my marvelous continent
just over there, releasing me
wrapped in a shroud.

I live, and from afar, I hear its swan song!

Peter Filkins

OSKAR PASTIOR

1927–

Dominotaurus

dominotaurusbekistandrogynecologistigmamasto
donauberginereidentaluminumbergenitalentrante
penultimathulethargypsychodramabelcantopicto
graphicalibertinagelatincanuterintesticularboreal
penstockmarkettlesterlinguanomenclavemariascle
piusageoldtimermaidenheadstarterrinebuchadnez
zarathustrapezebrandishwasherballustradebility
cooneandertalmudslidemiteflondonquixotempo
ratatouillerriennevapluperfectodermatitisepiano
stradamuscletterpressuresistancestralepharpoti
pharaocarinavigatoreador

Rosmarie Waldrop

HERTHA KRÄFTNER
1928–1951

On the Death of a Poet

My friend the poet is dead.
We buried him under an acacia tree.
His companion – a real shrew –
scrubbed the restaurant soup out of his tuxedo
(he wore it for the funeral)
because all his life, she said,
he had longed for purity.
She also thought the acacia smelled too strong,
he had always complained privately
about her heavy perfume.
She in turn had suffered, o, suffered she had
from his smell
of ink remover and stage dust
and cut-open paper and sometimes
– unfortunately – sometimes of a kind of powder
that she never used.
That's what his companion said
on the way home from the grave,
and that was all that could be said about his life.

Meanwhile he lay quietly under the sweet acacia tree.
If he had known it, he would have stayed up for nights
and tortured himself over some verses,
verses about white acacia blossoms
and a gray, moist morning
and bones bleaching under the grass.

Charlotte Melin

[124]

GÜNTER GRASS
1927–

Folding Chairs

How sad these changes are.
People unscrew the nameplates from the doors,
take the saucepan of cabbage
and heat it up again, in a different place.

What sort of furniture is this
that advertises departure?
People take up their folding chairs
and emigrate.

Ships laden with homesickness and the urge to vomit
carry patented seating contraptions
and their unpatented owners
to and fro.

Now on both sides of the great ocean
there are folding chairs;
how sad these changes are.

Michael Hamburger

In the Egg

We live in the egg.
We have covered the inside wall
of the shell with dirty drawings
and the Christian names of our enemies.
We are being hatched.

Whoever is hatching us
is hatching our pencils as well.

Set free from the egg one day
at once we shall draw a picture
of whoever is hatching us.

We assume that we're being hatched.
We imagine some good-natured fowl
and write school essays
about the colour and breed
of the hen that is hatching us.

When shall we break the shell?
Our prophets inside the egg
for a middling salary argue
about the period of incubation.
They posit a day called X.

Out of boredom and genuine need
we have invented incubators.
We are much concerned about our offspring inside the egg.
We should be glad to recommend our patent
to her who looks after us.

But we have a roof over our heads.
Senile chicks,
polyglot embryos
chatter all day
and even discuss their dreams.

And what if we're not being hatched?
If this shell will never break?
If our horizon is only that
of our scribbles, and always will be?
We hope that we're being hatched.

Even if we only talk of hatching
there remains the fear that someone

outside our shell will feel hungry
and crack us into the frying pan with a pinch of salt.
What shall we do then, my brethren inside the egg?

Michael Hamburger

Don't Turn Round

Don't go into the wood,
in the wood is the wood.
Whoever walks in the wood,
looks for trees,
will not be looked for later in the wood.

Have no fear,
fear smells of fear.
Whoever smells of fear
will be smelled out
by heroes who smell like heroes.

Don't drink from the sea,
the sea tastes of more sea.
Whoever drinks from the sea
henceforth feels
a thirst only for oceans.

Don't build a home,
or you'll be at home.
Whoever is at home
waits for
late callers and opens the door.

Don't write a letter,
archives will boast of letters you post.
Whoever writes the letter

lends his name
to the posthumous paper game.

Michael Hamburger

The Fortress Grows

The land lies fallow, food now for rooks and crows.
The moles proliferate and, as they'd never done,
suspect, along the fences strange dogs run.
We are to pay: in cash, and through the nose.

Because mid-European, wealthy and vulnerable,
fear sweated out its draughts for a defensive wall:
now as a fortress Novemberland seeks to be
safe from Black, Fellah, Jew, Turk, Romany.

As eastern border Poland will serve again:
so fast we think of history, to our gain.
Building of castles has always been our special joy,
to raise the rampart, excavate the moat;
and against fortress, megrims, dullness, gloom attacks
always a Hölderlin helped with poems in our packs.

Michael Hamburger

GÜNTER KUNERT
1929–

About Some Who Survived

When the man
was pulled out
from
under the debris
of his bombed house,
he shook himself
and said:
Never again

At least not right away.

Charlotte Melin

Film Put in Backwards

When I woke
I woke in the breathless black
Of the box.
        I heard: the earth
Was opening over me. Clods
Fluttered back
        To the shovel. The
Dear box, with me the dear
        Departed, gently rose.
The lid flew up and I
Stood, feeling:
        Three bullets travel
Out of my chest
Into the rifles of soldiers, who

                    Marched off, gasping
            Out of the air a song
            With calm firm steps
                    Backwards.

Christopher Middleton

Shelley Plain

for Wolfgang Koeppen

Deus absconditus lives under the eaves
opposite the englischer Garten
close to heaven. His door on the latch. A pilgrim
comes from afar. On a sofa salvaged from a skip
in the hallway lounges Cerberus, a tamed heathen
with black pelt and soft muzzle.
Then himself, unconcealed
in the guise of a badly shaved patriarch
with bewildered blinking smile
as his unmistakeable sign.
Powerful spectacles for eyes,
the better to see us with.
Feeble gesture of welcome. Shakes in the right hand.
A consequence of lonely evenings and much drinking.
No sooner had he caught sight of us than
a telephonic De Profundis rang out,
a frantic human appeal from the local exchange.
God put down the receiver,
in the stern pretence that we are all
created alike, in accordance with his inflexible
capriciousness
towards power and insistence.

Michael Hofmann

HEINER MÜLLER
1929–1995

Brecht

Truly, he lived in dark times.
The times have brightened.
The times have darkened.
When brightness says, I am darkness,
It has told the truth.
When darkness says, I am
Brightness, it does not lie.

Reinhold Grimm

The Hyena

The hyena loves the tanks stranded in the desert, because the
crews are dead. She can wait. She waits until the thousand
and first sandstorm has gnawed through the steel. Then her
hour has come. The hyena is the heraldic beast of mathematics, she knows there must be nothing left over. Her god is
zero.

Michael Hofmann

Heart of Darkness adapted from Joseph Conrad

For Gregor Gysi

Gruesome world capitalist world
– Gottfried Benn, in a radio interview with Johannes R. Becher, 1930

In the hard-currency-bar of the Hotel METROPOL
Berlin Capital of the GDR a Polish whore
A foreign worker is hitting
Up a very old man with a cold
Between the chapters of his lecture
About freedom in the U.S.A.
He snorts into a snot-rag and yells for the trash can
Still feeling pity for her difficult profession
I hear two travelling salesmen
Bavarian from the sound of it
Dividing up Asia: WELL I WOULD LIKE MALAYSIA
THAILAND KOREA TOO IS PART OF IT
WELL I WOULD ALSO PLAN THE CROSS-TRACK SYSTEM
FOR YEMEN THEN
THAT WOULD TAKE CARE OF IT

                   CHINA IS PART OF IT TOO
CHINA IS THE ONLY PROJECT THAT'S BEEN SOLD
In the elevated train ZOOLOGISCHER GARTEN
   FRIEDRICHSTRASSE
I came to know two citizens of the GDR
One of them says My son three weeks old
Was born with a sign in front of his chest
I WAS IN THE WEST ON THE NINTH OF NOVEMBER
My daughter same age I have twins
Carries the inscription ME TOO
THE HORROR THE HORROR THE HORROR

Margitt Lehbert

[132]

HANS MAGNUS ENZENSBERGER
1929–

the end of the owls

i speak for none of your kind,
i speak of the end of the owls.
i speak for the flounder and whale
in their unlighted house,
the seven-cornered sea,
for the glaciers
they will have calved too soon,
raven and dove, feathery witnesses,
for all those that dwell in the sky
and the woods, and the lichen in gravel,
for those without paths, for the colorless bog
and the desolate mountains.

glaring on radar screens,
interpreted one final time
around the briefing table, fingered
to death by antennas, floridas swamps
and the siberian ice, beast
and bush and basalt strangled
by earlybird, ringed
by the latest maneuvers, helpless
under the hovering firebells,
in the ticking of crises.

we're as good as forgotten.
don't fuss with the orphans,
just empty your mind
of its longing for nest eggs,
glory or psalms that won't rust.

i speak for none of you now,
all you plotters of perfect crimes,
nor for me, nor for anyone.
i speak for those who can't speak,
for the deaf and dumb witnesses,
for otters and seals,
for the ancient owls of the earth.

Jerome Rothenberg

karl heinrich marx

gigantic grandfather
jehovah-bearded
on brown daguerrotypes
i see your face
in the snow-white aura
despotic quarrelsome
and your papers in the linen press:
butcher's bills
inaugural addresses
warrants for your arrest

your massive body
i see in the 'wanted' book
gigantic traitor
displaced person
in tail coat and plastron
consumptive sleepless
your gall-bladder scorched
by heavy cigars
salted gherkins laudanum
and liqueur

i see your house
in the rue d'alliance
dean street grafton terrace
gigantic bourgeois
domestic tyrant
in worn-out slippers:
soot and 'economic shit'*
usury 'as usual'*
children's coffins
rumours of sordid affairs

no machine-gun
in your prophet's hand:
i see it calmly
in the british museum
under the green lamp
break up your own house
with a terrible patience
gigantic founder
for the sake of other houses
in which you never woke up

gigantic zaddik
i see you betrayed
by your disciples:
only your enemies
remained what they were:
i see your face
on the last picture
of april eighty-two:
an iron mask:
the iron mask of freedom

Michael Hamburger

* Quotations from Marx's letters to Engels in the 1850s and 1860s. *H.M.E.*

foam

at the hour of birth i was blinded with foam in my eyes
crying with grief unable to look at the sky
on a black friday thirty years in the past

foam hangs from the century's mouth foam
in the bank vaults foam howling
in the wombs of mothers in the lead-lined bunkers
foam in the pink-tinged bidets

no bolt from the blue can undo it: it flowers
it covers the length and breadth of the earth
with its maddening snot: no fire no sword
can stop it it's endless no fooling there's nothing
that does it no plan no hatchet no secret device
it's too sweet it rises up from the depths
and it foams it smirks and it foams

slip me a brotherly handshake you sellouts
your fingers flecked with warts shell fragments diamonds
subsisting on obscene subordinate clauses
deliver your adams apples to my judasbite
your foaming soap hearts and your bank accounts
stained red with haemoglobin: pull me down to the ground
as far down as you as the other gobs of phlegm
in that professional muck.

i'm here any day of the week a fire-eater like you
like everyone else: standing on my corner from nine
to five taking painful shots of my own fire
for ten bucks a day kneedeep in foaming status quo
between carburettors and street lights

hear o hear

who hollers god bless you out of the foam?
who tells me to hope? and what should i hope for?
who slips me a clammy brotherly handshake?

all right get off it i'm not one of you
i'm not one of us: i somehow got to be born
when the riot squads turned on the hoses: i somehow
started to howl no fooling alone without brothers blinded
on a black friday in a pink-tinged bidet

and why alone and why pink-tinged and why
not and why no fooling

who doesn't schluck his own fire? who
doesn't wade through piles of clipped fingernails?
who doesn't leave an oily loophole in his contracts?
who waits to be saved? and by whom? and from what?
who doesn't bolt endless food with sincerest best wishes?
who doesn't get taxed? who hasn't caught
the cry of fear at the stockholders meeting?

who doesn't have a lung made of plastic? okay then
who's ever been through a factory? who
hasn't got that smell in his throat? who
isn't divorced? and why not?
who's never sent a picture postcard from capri?
who doesn't fuck around with history?
who isn't sorry he's living? and why not?
and why not? who doesn't say and so forth?
and why and so forth? who hollers for help?
and why help? and why why?

who doesn't know that he's croaking? but why all the sweat
if nobody dies from it? who isn't a walking tachistoscope?
who doesn't have handcuffs on his mouth
and a saniflushed brain? but why all the sweat?

why all the sweat about royalty checks? and why not?
why all the sweat if the garbage cans blossom with
    peacocks
and mystical roses? no fooling why all the sweat?
why all the sweat with this foam?

o fire-eater with the heat turned off slip me some skin
o mummy in your mummy-cloth of pink-tinged foam
                              god bless you
deliver your bubbling gullet to my kow-tow
for behold i am one of you
i'd like to strangle you in your own foam
because i somehow still happen to be living
somehow i'm tough as some old cripple
who calls himself no man who somehow
gets by and won't die from it: tough
and without an address and cold as the sky

so get going get moving what are you waiting here for?
for the el-train maybe? for the non-reparations?
for the tax-deductible deluge?

the fix is on the last judgment
company cars deliver the popes
in their foam-flecked tiaras

over red-hot telephone wires brokers are bobbing their
    heads
in the sweat of their pig-leather faces:
the class struggle's ended the victim's
sprawled on the floor in his fat:
liquid holdings: foam in the rose-colored eyes
moldy banners and barricades wrapped in cellophane
propped in the showcase: while from an antique jukebox
the internationale drones: a beat rock and roll

the chiefs of staff play golf out in space
beyond the sound barrier progress
reviews the ranks of its housebroken scientists
castrated cashiers in the federal reserve sing.
arias dripping with foam: till the rapturous clubwomen
peel the chinchilla wraps from their deep-frozen bosoms

cadillacs tear gas and barracks
for africa s & h stamps
for the free world's waterlogged bellies

and why not give prizes for tits? hollywood
ass in the rose-colored foam: striptease
of the western world from dortmund to san diego

no fooling why not? and why not build
launching pads? should our kids maybe
have things better than us? why all the sweat?

why all the sweat when the prize lodgers crawl under the
    rugs
and take bites out of the woodwork and chew up the want
    ads?
why all the sweat? and what can we do with them? what
    can we do with the widows?
what can we do with the communists? what can we do with
    everyone
who says hölderlin and means himmler with everyone
who pays off rockets and cops in installments who makes
    movies
and fucks and connects? what can we do with the
    archbishops?

what can we do with the unemployed geniuses who fall
whimpering out of their windows? get them out get them
    out in the rain

[139]

in the deep rancid foam in the madhouses
in the prisons in the lobbies of congress
where the spit of liars runs down the walls
and where else? in the cast iron crematoria maybe
or just let them rot down at customs: at the
goddamn bureau the goddamn bureau the goddamn
   bureau of customs

and what can we do with ourselves? and the crowds
that fill up the football stadiums crying
for coca colas and bloodbaths: what can we do with them?
what can we do with god? what can we do with his
holy likeness sitting there gobbling up glass splinters?
volunteer him into the army: into the foam

into the maddening black and pink foam
into the whinnying foam-sloshing foam

let go get your hands off: i'm somehow still living
i somehow got to be born
and i know this taste of chlorine and lead
can't you sniff it under the whipped cream?
you stiffs that keep lapping it up in your coffins
heil hitler god bless you: this taste
of auschwitz in the cafe flore in doney's:
of budapest in the savoy: of johannesburg where?

and why and so forth? and why the birth
of some bloody quintuplets right there in the papers?
the eruptions of turbulent ancient volcanoes?
these coronations and riots? the hell with it
ditch it no fooling: these spring floods
that none of you die from: you die on the can
when you realize that men eat each other
no fooling: that each man gobbles his neighbour

and why not? why no gingerbread hearts?
and no free market tips for the council of churches?
so okay why no mocha? why no coma?
why no amuck? nobody dies from it
you die in nato no fooling from too much fat
in your hearts: in a cabal of acolytes
in a foam-rubber skyscraper in düsseldorf
you die on the can no fooling
when you realize just who you are

so buy your air-conditioned coffins with the built-in toilets
verily verily price going up whoops
you wind up with a throat full of steel wool
what are you waiting for? stuff the diamonds in
under your shirt: shove the can opener in and the
   harpsichord
shake your nemesis down for a lump sum payment
and pack your bags pack the securities in
pack in your gasmasks pack in your bellies
buy geiger counters and old masters
buy little boys and bequeath them
your juice while it lasts
buy up monday buy up the ocean
buy up branflakes and bombs buy
the geniuses out at the airport
buy poison and wait till i
smear it over your affluent tongues
(it'll kill you or give you a charge)
buy up some kulcher and roll it around on your gums
like a life-saver: play the crummy swiss market
sit tight why not? sell out stand pat
cash in sign over pay off

and why not? why no headhunters
in furlined convertibles? why no vats
full of monkey glands for the fancy clinics?
who here should throw the first stone?

who doesn't live through the mainline? who hasn't cracked
open a skull at the crossroads? so okay
who isn't mixed up with the international mucous
    membrane cartel?
who doesn't know what waschzwang is? who isn't called
    pilate?

open up ditch it enter the federal fuzz the marriage guest
    cometh
the congressional medal of honor steps forth: the mixed
    chorus the latest statistics
the heavenly bridegroom and the general strike
open the gas-jets amen fear and tremble

god bless you: head for the bars for the brink start singing
bis dat qui cito dat gold help you: flags up
si vis pacem para bellum strip down sprawl out
in saecula saeculorum

they won't stop they die a little bit more every minute
but never completely they talk dumb they go on and on
about doomsday: with the pointer at zero
they still slop their caviar still splatter
egg white over the walls of their cell
faretheewell my honey my intercontinental fart
    faretheewell
they breaststroke up rivers of gin and chanel
smelling of foam and clogged pipes it's too much!

it's mad: no bolt from the blue can undo them
no rilkes can save them no diors they stink

[142]

to high heaven while bach weeks screech from the jukebox
they wear masks made of mayonnaise and putty
they stand in the shadow of death still killing each other
with fire extinguishers gas pipes and inter-office reports

let go! ditch it! from this i know nothing
i'm not one of us i'm not one of anyone
keep off with your hands i'm alone let go

i don't want to change you god help you
it leaves me cold it's really too mad
o brothers in foam o prelates o eaters of fire
o boards of directors sprung from the waves i'm watching
    you
cooling it thinking it out for myself asking
verily verily where will it end with you?
foam-blinded soap hearts where will it end? and why
down in hell? and why not? and what makes you
scream for johann sebastian? and what
gives you noses like mine? and why should the future
be foaming so sweetly? a blood clot away out
in the rose-colored sky

okay call me no man: say that i'm no man's kid brother
from no man's land let me break loose so at least
i can rest from all these live people:
let's make out that i'm not one of you that i'm not one of us
that i'm free from all that, from us, from this foam,

this snivelling smirking sweet-tasting foam
that hangs from the century's mouth that rises

higher and higher and swells in the bank vaults
that smells in the honeymoon beds in your poems and
why not? in my own foam-flecked heart

[143]

while it swims around blinded in boiling foam
and gets rusty and swims
immortal as a paper clip

further and further

into the rose-colored future

Jerome Rothenberg

In Memory of William Carlos Williams

In his last year, he was all but blind,
cheerful and peculiar,
expressed no opinions, didn't watch
the tube, didn't read
any reviews,
neither *Look* nor *Life*.

No 'representative figure,'
country doctor in Rutherford, N.J.
No gala dinners *chez* Kennedy:
a wooden veranda,
'smeared a bluish green that,
weathered, faded, pleases me better
than all other colors.'

For the Stockholm Academy
not quite right,
for the reporters unprofitable,
not blind enough for *Look*,
too alive for *Life*
with his eighty years
he perceived more in his backyard
than all of New York over twelve channels:

chickens and sick people,
the light and the darkness.

Took off his glasses:
'The plums in the icebox so sweet and cold' and
'The tread of the old man gathering dog-lime
is more majestic
than that of the Episcopal minister on Sunday.'

Saw the darkness and the light,
did not forget the chickens,
was precise
and peculiarly cheerful.

Reinhold Grimm and Felix Pollak

Identity Check

This is not Dante.
This is a photograph of Dante.
This is a film showing an actor who pretends to be Dante.
This is a film with Dante in the role of Dante.
This is a man who dreams of Dante.
This is a man called Dante who is not Dante.
This is a man who apes Dante.
This is a man who passes himself off as Dante.
This is a man who dreams that he is Dante.
This is a man who is the very spit image of Dante.
This is a wax figure of Dante.
This is a changeling, a double, an identical twin.
This is a man who believes he is Dante.
This is a man everybody, except Dante, believes to be Dante.

This is a man everybody believes to be Dante, only he
    himself does not fall for it.
This is a man nobody believes to be Dante, except Dante.
This is Dante.

H.M.E.

At Thirty-three

It was all so different from what she'd expected.
Always those rusting Volkswagens.
At one time she'd almost married a baker.
First she read Hesse, then Handke.
Now often she does crosswords in bed.
With her, men take no liberties.
For years she was a Trotskyist, but in her own way.
She's never handled a ration card.
When she thinks of Kampuchea she feels quite sick.
Her last lover, the professor, always wanted her to beat him.
Greenish batik dresses, always too wide for her.
Greenflies on her *Sparmannia*.
Really she wanted to paint, or emigrate.
Her thesis, *Class Struggles in Ulm 1500*
to 1512 and References to them in Folksong:
Grants, beginnings and a suitcase full of notes.
Sometimes her grandmother sends her money.
Tentative dances in her bathroom, little grimaces,
cucumber juice for hours in front of the mirror.
She says, whatever happens I shan't starve.
When she weeps she looks like nineteen.

Michael Hamburger

The Holiday

Now that he's free, relatively, often he shuffles
round the tennis courts, pays for a shave, reads.
Black marketeers whisper, plimsolls pant past him.
Stiff with palm trees, the world expands
on Sundays. Here, in the Palace, the first whores
brood over their breakfast. All is clear, all fuzzes.
Well, if it isn't Nick! comes from the next table.
On the beach, howling misery. Complications
melt away pesetas. Chance acquaintances,
longingly primed with lotion. 'What do you say, José,
if tonight we go and play? Olé, olé, olé.'
Disgusting, this platter of octopus.
The yawning bedroom. Sand in the towels.
A brilliant insect that collides with the lightbulb.
Seventeen across: Greek fertility goddess.
The shower smells musty. In the street someone titters.
Motorbikes rev. Then there's only the sea
that sighs away into the distance. No, it's the next room,
in the next room a woman is dying or loving herself.
Olé, olé what do you say, José? He listens.
White in his tooth-glass the sleeping tablets teem.

Michael Hamburger

Visiting Ingres

Today he'd be painting for the Central Committee, or
    Paramount,
it all depends. But at that time a gangster still sweated
under his ermine, and the con-men had themselves
    crowned.

[147]

So let's have them, the insignia, the pearls, the peacock
    feathers.

We find the artist pensive. He has stuffed himself
with 'choice ideas and noble passions'.
A laborious business. Expensive small armchairs, First or
    Second Empire,
it all depends. Soft chin, soft hands, 'Hellas in his soul'.

For sixty years this cold greed, every inch a craftsman,
till he's achieved it: fame, the rosette in his buttonhole.

These women, writhing in front of him on the marble
like seals made of risen dough: between thumb and
    forefinger
the breasts measured, the surface studied like plush,
tulle, glossy taffeta, the moisture in the corner of their eyes
glazed twelve times over like gelatine, the flesh colour
    smooth
and narcotic, better than Kodak: exhibited
in the Ecole des Beaux-Arts, a venal eternity.

What's it all for? What for the tin of his decorations,
the fanatical industry, the gilt plaster eagles?

Curiously bloated he looks at eighty,
worn out, with that top hat in his left hand.
'It was all for nothing'. How can you say that, most
    honoured Maître!
What will the frame-maker think of you, the glazier?
your faithful cook, the undertaker? His only answer:

A sigh. Far above the clouds, oniric, the fingers of Thetis
that squirm like worms on Jupiter's black beard.
Reluctantly we take a last brief look

at the artist – how short his legs are! –
and tiptoe out of the studio.

Michael Hamburger

Valse triste et sentimentale

Blast the old days.
What about now?
Do as you like,
but please,
no apologies.

You did, didn't you?
With or without it.
Or else
you didn't.
That's all there is to it.

'What do you want me to do?
What do you want me to do?'
Of course. I know.
That's what they all ask
when it's too late.

A pity, really.
Sometimes I begin to miss you
with your eternal scenes,
your foggy excuses,
your hocus pocus.

Me, feeling guilty?
You make me laugh.
Get out of here

and don't show your face again,
ever.

H.M.E.

Fetish

All night
he is thinking of it
a wisp of down
smaller
than the hand of a man
There is nothing else
he can think of
there is nothing
but this tuft of hair
which is not here
He imagines it
dark
a woolly mass
curling
brightly
He can almost hear it
rustle
at the touch of his hand
He sees it
bristling
in the light
blonde black
soft and unruly
glittering madly
and scarcely worth
further notice

H.M.E.

In Memory of Sir Hiram Maxim (1840–1916)

I (1945)

On the way to school in the ditch,
the roar of the fighter-plane swooping down,
little clouds of dust to the left, in front of us,
to the right, soundless, and only a moment later
the aircraft gun's hammering.
We did not appreciate his invention.

II (1854–1878)

Later, much later did he emerge
from an old encyclopaedia. A country boy.
Their farm in the wilderness, harassed
by bears, a long time ago. At fourteen,
a cartwright's apprentice. Sixteen hours a day
at four dollars a month. Scraped along
as a brass-founder, boxer, instrument maker,
shouting: A chronic inventor, that's me!
Improved mousetraps and curlers
and built a pneumatic merry-go-round.
His steam aeroplane, with a boiler
of 1200 pounds, three tons water-supply,
broke down under its own dead weight.
Neither did his ersatz coffee take off.
He had to wait for the Great Paris Exhibition,
a fairy-world of arc-lamps and filaments,
for the Legion of Honour and for his illumination.

III (1881–1901)

Three years later the Prince of Wales
could inspect in the vaults of Hatton Garden

a miracle of precision:
it loaded, cocked, bolted and triggered,
opened the breech-lock, ejected the shell,
reloaded, cocked, again and again, by itself,
and the cadence was fabulous: ten rounds
per second, continuous firing.
The recoil barrel, a stroke of genius!
cried the Duke of Cambridge. Never again
will war be what it used to be!
A weapon of unprecedented elegance!
The knighthood was not long in coming.

IV (1994)

Nowadays of course, with his masterpiece
being available in any school playground,
we fail to feel what he must have felt:
the compulsive joy of a bearded mammal
with 270 patents to his credit.
As to us, his juniors by a hundred years,
we lay low as if dead in the ditch.

H.M.E.

Autumn 1944

True, to the one who lay in the grass
they seemed glorious,
glittering there so high up
against the cloudless October sky,
the bomber chains, and he didn't care
about those mementos
that far away were burnt
in the mouldering loft:

antique cups and angel's hair,
Grandfather's postcards from Paris
(Oh là là) and his belt buckle
from another war,
petticoats with holes, decorations,
dolls' houses, the Psyche in plaster
and a few forgotten proofs of God
in a cigar-box –

but those corpses in the cellar
are still there.

Michael Hamburger

His Father's Ghost

Some evenings he sits there
as he used to do, slightly bowed,
humming at his table
under the iron lamp.
The Chinese ink pen skims
the graph paper.
Quietly, sure of itself,
it traces its black course.
At times he listens to me,
his snow-white hair inclined,
absently smiles, goes on drawing
towards his wondrous plan
which I cannot understand,
which he'll never complete.
I hear him hum.

Michael Hamburger

Gazetteer

Pity about the Dragon Kingdom Druk-Yul
that hardly anyone could find on a map
and about the Republic of Our Saviour
with its grey-haired raiding parties;
and more still a pity about the desperate Democratic
and Popular Republic of Algeria;
a pity also, though for other reasons,
about the Confoederatio Helvetica
littered with bank statements and needles –
worries not to be likened to
the tribulations of the Homeland of Peace
and the Republic of Honourable Men;
a pity, a neverending pity about the Federal Republic
of Jugoslavia with all its stricken
once autonomous regions;
a pity, though for other reasons,
about the United States of America
and its numerous inhabitants who,
each man for himself, skulking in their garages
clutch at their personalised shotguns;
a pity, in God's name, about Abu Dhabi Dubai Ash-Shariqah
Ra's al-Khaymah Al-Fujayrah Umm al-Qaywayn and
    Ajman,
The United Arab Emirates! a pity too
a pity, though to a lesser degree,
about the Federal Republics of Germany and Micronesia,
yes, even about the Most Serene Republic of San Marino
groaning under its souvenir shops
and about the Hellenic Republic that cannot be comforted
and the troubled and burdened Medinat Yisra'el;
to say nothing of the immeasurably distressed

Russian Federation
and the far more immeasurable
Zhongua Renmin Gongheguo;
and alas, alas for the red, green and clay-coloured
République Rwandaise and its 6211518
inmates left, and likewise many another
region enveloped in sackcloth and ashes
we rarely think about.

David Constantine

Druk Yul, Bhutan; *Republic of Our Saviour*, El Salvador; *Homeland of Peace*,
Myanmar, formerly Burma; *Republic of Honourable Men*, Burkina Faso; *Medinat
Yisra'el*, Israel; *Zhonghua Renmin Gonghheguo*, China.

ADOLF ENDLER

1930–

When the war was over:

There was a nest of blood red swallow down,
there was a nest, built with the naked bones
of little swallows that wanted to live
in this nest built with their little bones,
so warm in the nest of their down blood red.

Charlotte Melin

JÜRGEN BECKER
1932–

Changing Wind

Paestum. Or was the reference to Birra Peroni . . . No one
knew anything at the goulash/ mattress party; who was
Raymond Roussel –

                shadows of obscure words

                                  (un-
noticed)
        drift off. Memory sealed shut.
Who drove the blue Volkswagen, at the end of

                                  what
short story? in the rain . . .

                    But the salad days
of shellac records; the novelty of old sounds;
and the roads won't be

                empty and dark
changing wind for comparison: wind
in the mutation of metaphor

                      (the end of metaphor, or:
objective in the new teaching of German).

                        Most don't notice
anything
        (something's afoot); a few have already taken it
upon themselves to leave; others are silent and hesitating.

Michael Hofmann

Hotel Belgica

The cook is doing the crossword.
Wouldn't mind helping, blonde,
don't speak any Flemish.
Cod in white sauce was pretty good.
Her girls all smoke too much.
Another beer, one more.
Tonight's stormy, just like
last night; now the dictionary.
Will anyone else come,
sailor, hotel guest, ghost.
You are still beautiful; ageing
wood panelled walls, benches and mirrors.
Exploitrix, smile, why don't you?
Here the day before yesterday too,
more beer, same table.
Do you hear it, crashing outside,
the surf, or whatever it is.
Letters, words; I've no Flemish
and I'll never learn now, one more beer
in this night without words.

Michael Hofmann

'. . . Funerals in summer'

. . . Funerals in summer. No let-up now.
You meet acquaintances, and after ten years
of not seeing each other, you always start off
on the wrong foot, with mistaken identities:
at least you're still able to make the exit
under your own steam. The world champion, 19,

moans about feeling her age, and you have water-lilies
in a crap poem. There are certain regions
you'd better stop going to; your village has got prettier,
the vicarage has cable now, and the man
who ran the chip shop has bunked off to Lanzarote.
Surprise, there are a few vacancies in the old cemetery.
the funeral feast is next door, at that handy Italian's . . .

Michael Hofmann

Autumn Story

A drawing, or just a scribble . . . I had tried
to prop up the old collapsing pear tree.
But the prop of pencil lines didn't hold up.
For a few days now, it's been all fog,
which finally today has obscured all visibility.
This is how it is every year, structures,
frosts, owl flight, wars in September.

Michael Hofmann

The Bringers of Beethoven

for Ludvik Kundera

They set out to bring Beethoven
to everyone.
And as they had a record with them
they played for speedier understanding
Symphony no. 5, in C minor, opus 67

But the man M. said
it was too loud for him, he
was getting old

In the night the bringers of Beethoven put
up poles in streets and squares
hooked up cables, connected
loudspeakers, and with the dawn
for more thorough acquaintance came the strains of
Symphony no. 5, in C minor, opus 67,
came loud enough to be heard
in the mute fields.

But the man M. said he had a headache,
went home about noon, closed
doors and windows and praised
the thickness of the walls

Thus provoked, the bringers of Beethoven strung
wire on to the walls and hung
loudspeakers over the windows, and in
through the panes came
Symphony no. 5, in C minor, opus 67

But the man M. stepped out of the house and denounced
the bringers of Beethoven;
they all asked him what he had
against Beethoven

Thus attacked, the bringers of Beethoven knocked
on M.'s door and when they opened up they
forced a foot inside; praising the neatness of the place
they went in.
The conversation happened to turn
to Beethoven,
and to enliven the subject they happened
to have with them
Symphony no. 5, in C minor, opus 67

But the man M. hit the bringers of
Beethoven with an iron ladle.
He was arrested just in time.

M.'s act was called homicidal
by lawyers and judges of the bringers of Beethoven.
But they must not give up hoping.
He was sentenced
to Symphony no. 5, in C minor, opus 67,
by Ludwig van Beethoven

M. kicked and screamed,
until the loudspeakers stopped
beyond the mute fields

He was just too old, the bringers of Beethoven said.
But by M.'s coffin, they said,
are his children

And his children demanded
that over the coffin of

the man M. should be played
Symphony no. 5, in C minor, opus 67

Gordon and Gisela Brotherston

With the Volume Turned Down

Then came
twelve years
when I wasn't allowed to publish
says the man on the radio

I think of X
and start counting

Ewald Osers

In Memoriam Johannes Bobrowski

His photograph
on the hoardings

Now

His papers have been
examined, the poet is
reassuringly dead

Ewald Osers

SARAH KIRSCH

1935–

Sad Day

I am a tiger in the rain
water parts my hide
drops drop into my eyes

I shuffle slowly, slide my paws
along Friedrichstrasse
and am stone-broke in the rain

I fight my way through cars on red
walk into the café for bitters
eat the band and swing out

I bellow sharply at the rain on Alex-Platz
the high-rise gets wet, loses its belt
(I snarl: one does what one can)

But it rains the seventh day
Then I'm angry up to the eyelashes

I hiss the street empty
and sit down among honest seagulls

They all look left into the Spree

And when I mighty tiger howl
they understand: I mean there should
still be other tigers here

Wayne Kvam

Winter

I learn to know myself, at present
the lodging that saw
at least three generations of people,
always the windows had
an arch above, the sills small
hardly suited to foliage in pots
the walls
like annual rings of trees
bear layers of wallpaper
on the bottom Jugendstil, in between
wastepaper newspaper reports
enraged readers on brothels
two lines Reichstag's fire then
only more wallpaper, the handicraft
slackened. Or the outlook
onto roofs (hardly a piece of sky) they
had that before me in their view, likely
similar rain and snow blackened
the asphalt in the yard made the masonry red
others
are still to see it, a cat
has accompanied me a few years what
does she know of me she loves my perfume
or simply the spot on which
I'm sitting I am not very good, but
learned patience at water-coloring when
I was little:
if one doesn't wait, one loses the picture –
and sometimes
my heart moves in its suspension bands
that is, when I see a strange countryside

hear of courageous people or
someone asks a question;
I love my peasant's fur my boots
and my sad face

Wayne Kvam

Alone

The old women before red houses
Red hydrangea crippled trees
Brought me tea. Worthily
They carried the trays back, resumed
Listening- and observation posts
Behind tittle-tattle-ornamental curtains.

Wayne Kvam

Letter

I am happy in Italy, in this
Early December. Mornings the stars, then
Fog under the green trees. The stone bird
Clinks pebbles together with his voice, you see me
On red tiles and although
The stove is an electric stove I do
The simple things of three hundred years past.
I roast – yes I have seen Pompeii and two thousand
Pillars and all the churches, secluded gardens – I roast
The rabbit in a pot and he gets
A whiskey after and I too I have
The writing stuff on the kitchen table and live and live
And live still and my lover

Has curls and clothes of velvet and silk and fine
Eight-footed hounds, they bring
Me boots and light and fire, something to smoke and then
Comes himself

Wayne Kvam

CHRISTOPH MECKEL
1935–

from Acid

And I'm still waiting for you to come up
                                        from the coast in that
clapped out bus that stops here once a day
        and drops loads of people that no one's waiting for.
Your suitcases have come, your scarves, your shoes
        and the coloured glasses that we stole on the Rialto
the bed is here, and your robe, and death never left,
only you're missing, your breathing, your laughter, for two.

                                *

Her telephone number. When I finally lost her,
            I thought: well, you're shot of that at least:
standing around in a callbox in winter, and you've gained
                                something: time
and winter in loose handfuls
quiet in a dark bar over a sherry
            and Iris takes off on a rainbow.
All right; then I find it in my jacket pocket
two weeks later, and the whole thing starts over again:
yes, no, maybe
                        the whole purring inferno.

                                *

End of summer, and Julia left this morning
            with someone by the name of Hopkins.
By the time she comes back, shattered
        and weepy, she'll have lost her dark sweet, moist,
    fragrant mouth

and will no longer be reckoned among the beautiful things.
The end, as always, is brought about by some Hopkins or
   other.

*

I found the belt of her red
              dressing-gown under the stairs long after she
  was gone,
and at night. I hadn't expected any more
low blows.
                     Imagine, having to start a life
  with nothing
and a belt.

*

Years of sleep, uselessness
              and forgetting.
Then one day: her face in the clear morning sky
her bare shoulders, smell of coffee
             and the leaves on the stairs
an old cigarette lighter in a wellington boot
laughter for no reason
        the cries of the jackdaws filling the valley
        screams of the jackdaws filling a lifetime.

Michael Hofmann

KURT BARTSCH
1937–

Tears

When the unpleasant character
Of the deceased
Was made known
Some mourners felt ashamed
Of the tears they had shed
At his graveside and claimed
They had been weeping for joy.

Michael Hofmann

G.

My sister with her head in the gas oven.
What was going through her mind as she died.
What was going through her mind when she was alive.
I think the world didn't make any particular
Impression on her in forty years.
War hunger cold. Two children, her husband
a drunk. She loves him, though. He lives
off her back, off the work she performs quietly,
like a quiet animal. When he leaves her,
she twice tries to do away with herself.
The third time she is successful.
On the gravestone, it says she was alive.

Michael Hofmann

A Visit from Enzensberger

Position 52′ 31″ North, 13′ 25″ East,
on my sofa Herr Enzensberger
is wearing a cutaway, a touch of *fin de siècle*
in deference to the future, I have a sense of something white
floating in his eyes (which are light-blue),
and I remember thinking how prettily
the sugar is reflected in them, on the silver
tongs, when I hear a faint tinkle. A creak,
a scrape, what do I know. Then silence.
We smile. We drink tea. It's 19.43
Central European Time, outside the window
everything, even the snow, is black. WE ADVISE
YOU TO INQUIRE NO FURTHER.
BY ACTING OR FAILING TO ACT
YOU ARE MAKING YOURSELF PUNISHABLE.
I don't know why, a great feeling of peace
comes over me. There is, I see,
no iceberg in sight. The beginning of the end,
says Enzensberger, is always discreet.

Michael Hofmann

Question Answer Question
for Volker Braun

Why am I painting the walls?
I don't want to go on living here.
When the paint's all finished up,
I'll be on my way, I say. Oh,
why go to so much trouble, I ask
with a canny smile. So that,

when I go, I don't leave behind
something uninhabitable,
no sinking ship, as deserted by
proverbial rats. Then why
if it's so habitable, are you leaving?

Michael Hofmann

Market Position

What's going on?
The dogs are carrying on like crazy
today.
It takes the movements of the janitor's wife
to restore torpor.

In the market there's life
all the fresh vegetables and herbs
are there to be bought.
The fish-stall is closed
but a great array of fresh meat.
Tropical fruit cheaper
snaky cucumbers lettuces cheaper
amazing how bananas
are just being given away.
Cabbages cheap tomatoes dear
bell peppers almost gone
endives not for another two weeks.

The empty bottles
have to be stacked the winter clothes
pulled out. Soon
top buttons will be done up.
The dogs stray
cars spend longer parked in the dark.
In the first snow old ladies
walk at the side of old gentlemen.

Curious thing winter
before it's there.

Michael Hofmann

Self-Portrait

Often thought of as stout
and well-set
with a fluent gift for life
but I breakfast alone
after uneventful
dreams.
I my trouble
with hair-loss and sore feet
six-two and the son of a civil servant
indispensable to myself
not for sale I know
my worth a tad too exactly
and make love and poems on the side.
My face dilapidated
to best advantage in halflight
and in serious discussions.
I cigarette smoker half ash myself
drinker of coffee with elderly ladies
who help me out
on account of my pleasant expression and
my ruthless deployment
of good manners.

Michael Hofmann

ELKE ERB
1938–

Grimm's Fairytales

A grey sow in a corner. After a long walk in muddy shoes, after an already endless ride in the local, freezing, in a corner of the yard, at the end of the world, why don't you show us your animals, Karl, there she stands in the pale light, peers over the fence posts, a grey sow, in a low pen, at the end of the world.

Rosmarie Waldrop

N.'s Identity

'Situation!!' – Friedrich Hebbel, *Diaries*

N.'s wife had, even before the war, left him and married somebody else. The destruction of Dresden turned his street into rubble and ashes, later into a field. A bombing of Nordhausen murdered N.'s parents. Both his sisters died flee-ing, God knows where, they had no children. One friend was gassed, another was and remained missing. His brother fell in Holland. N. himself was a prisoner of war in England. He had helped build villas, not a single one remained standing. The only thing that, after the war, reminded us of N., was N.

Rosmarie Waldrop

VOLKER BRAUN

1939–

O Chicago! O Dialectic!

Now, Brecht, did you let your cigar go out?
In the course of the earthquakes we provoked
In those states that were built on sand.
Socialism takes its hat, never mind, here's Johnnie Walker.
I can't grab it by its principles
Which are falling out anyway. The warm streets
Of October are the chilly routes
Of market economics, Horatio. I wedge my gum in my cheek
And there it is, your nothing-much-worth-mentioning.

Michael Hofmann

The Theatre of the Dead

The dead conduct themselves the way they always do.
At night they step out onto the graveyard at Rotoli
For ritual exchanges of weapons and words. It's all they know.
The blood drains away into the Mediterranean. They erect
     ruins
CARTHAGE NEW YORK. The colossal
Left elbow of Jupiter in the museum at Tunis
He needed both of them to secure victory.
If only the living would . . . never mind.
YUPPY RABBLE. ALL THEY WANT IS THEIR MOUTHS
     STUFFED WITH SOMETHING TASTY
And game over. In general, I'm of the opinion
That socialism must be destroyed, and
I like my causes lost.

Michael Hofmann

[175]

Landscape

1 soot-covered tree
of a type no longer ascertainable
1 wrecked car
1 manmade wall, soundproofed

various defunct shoes
in the leafless shrubs

'what do you think you're doing there?'

1 essay, one excursion into biology
the quest for caddis fly larvae, the yellow

light of 6 p.m.

1 pair of stones

1 warning sign 'Private'
1 fly-tipped rotten sofa
1 sports plane

several fleeing animals,
the rest of a pair of stockings on
a bough, next to

1 rusty bicycle frame

1 recollection of
1 Zen joke

Michael Hofmann

KARIN KIWUS
1942–

Hommes à femme

When a small inconspicuous woman
delivers long, clever, and slightly
lisping speeches
about Don Juan and Casanova
then these men just get up
and hiss forchristsake and
what's the point of it all –
she's too much of a shrimp anyhow

Charlotte Melin

MICHAEL KRÜGER
1943–

Footnote

We're coming back to fetch
what remains: pillow; pillow-case; pall;
a drawing which hung unprotected
above the stove: *Hermes, the Guide
of the Dead* who, for the space of four years,
added spice to our meals. God has still
not been born; the clock stays hanging there;
so, in the hall, does the mirror. How
the flat grows and grows, the more it
empties, and how small is Time,
brooding away in the tomb-like rooms.
All is now dark, we've
removed the lamps: everything
passes softly through us. From where
my writing-desk once was,
I try to decipher a note
on the wall: Your Anger is Love.
A footnote in the history
of vanity, still to be written.

Richard Dove

Ernst Meister in Memoriam

In things
the eyes, Ernst,
prior to language.
Wherever you are

you return:
stone, threshold, house
are watching you closely.
Therefore, Ernst,
you remain alive,
always in view.

Richard Dove

JÜRGEN THEOBALDY
1944–

My Young Life

I want to grow up as big
as the men, when they rub their
thumbs on their suspenders.
The smoke of cigarettes mixes
with the dust of torn-down ruins
and the blue swaths of gases from BASF*
that drift over from Ludwigshafen.
Near the fairgrounds the Traber family suspends
a line from house to house and shows you how to make it
gracefully through the postwar years.
Below wind-down gradually the songs
of the working class, the red flags
disappear in the crowd, and
the union leaders look at their watches.
The television runs without sound
the whole afternoon already, now it's
the chaste sheriff's turn and thank god
he doesn't let himself get hooked
by this artful lady from Boston.
If I'm ever born again,
I want to come to the world
as a cigarette and then
burn out slowly between your lips.
While the television is still on,
in the bedroom my cousin shows me
her pussy. The pink uvula
between its lips is a discovery

* BASF – Badische Anilyn und Soda Fabrik, a chemical factory.

that I can't keep to myself.
A letter from the teacher, which
all my relatives read, threatens me
with reform school. Uncle Karl comes from nightshift,
eats his potato salad, plays the banker,
and wins for the first time in his life.
If this were a film, we would have
murdered him just after midnight. Dear Uncle Karl,
all in all we were a peaceful
family. Now we are pretty much apart,
my cousin got a divorce
and Cousin Willy too. Greetings
from Austria, the weather is beautiful.
My mother brings me a ballpoint pen
on which a little ship keeps
sailing on Wolfgangsee. In BASF
a cauldron explodes, and each worker
gets his own grave, although no one knows
which pieces from whom lay in it.
Uncle Karl still lives and takes me along
to the grave-rows. They remind me
of the war, I decide
to become a pacifist and listen to Pete Seeger
records. But before that, it's the Kirmes festival,
we hide in the darker passages of the
funhouse and smooch the girls
who always come in twos. Today they work
at BASF or at Daimler-Benz in Waldhof,
their breasts are grown larger, their behinds,
their arms. I hear from the business section
of the FAZ* that the firm where I apprenticed has

* FAZ – Frankfurter Allgemeine Zeitung, a conservative newspaper.

gone bankrupt: Back then it seemed so much bigger than
    me,
and now I've outlived it. Dear cousin,
all of us put together are still poorer
than every one of its stockholders. They change
their investments, you change arch-supports
and look for a new job. I already
quit in 1963 and go for the first time
to Paris. It is a sensation.
Hans and I find two whores for 17 francs,
afterwards we drink red wine at the counter,
talk about Rimbaud and from now on imagine
how really far out our life will be.

    Mitch Cohen

JOACHIM SARTORIUS
1946–

Alexandria

Back there is where he once sat, at this marble table,
said the old waiter, under the old-fashioned ventilators
that slowly revolved even in his lifetime,
under this ceiling with its art nouveau stucco,
la vie etait confortable: Stanley Beach,
Glymenopoulo, and the pleasant little
Cicinia, a cinema today, where they gave Tosca
in season, and la Bohème and Lohengrin
(the only Wagner that was then found acceptable
south of Naples). There he sat, a Greek,
one of a couple of tens of thousands of Greeks,
steadfastly ignoring half a million Egyptians.
He lived in an imaginary Europe,
that stopped with Strabo: 'the most magnificent
emporium in the inhabited world,'
which is now nothing but stone and sea,
and a feeling of millennial exhaustion.

Michael Hofmann

Vieux Jeu

To every traveller
his wizened leather frog
to every café
its sotto voce argument
to every cat
its mouse-life under the box tree

to every barber
his own sharpening antics

To every one:
his own market seller
with her grapes sweeter than anyone's.

Michael Hofmann

UWE KOLBE
1957–

Metamorphosis

I could be a wooden floor
I'd have no problem being a wooden floor or
Cobblestonecolored as the street or its dirt.
Or I could be the man in the suit
With the stiff knees and the whey face
I could be the girl running away from him
I could fall asleep in the subway
And be the official in the gaudy uniform
In the service of a higher power and throw
The bum out and get the cleaning woman
To mop up the up-chuck.
I could be the plastic floor, I dunno,
Would you still recognize me?
The man from Borges' story with the brain
That everything enters and nothing leaves.
I'd be happy with that and would fly away
From the windowsill along the street
In pursuit of it, then pass along
A friendly picture to a friendly female voice.
I would try to live with it to paint it
Black paint like all the devils under the cross.
I would be this great master with the
Almost imperceptible hand I'd have
Myself in my power would follow every fashion
Every tyrants' wisdom I Uwe Kolbe
Have all these possibilities open
Those of the little daily fascist
Those of the confused of the sculpture of the stage.

Happily too happily the fairytale figure too
Instead of three golden hairs the hard phrase.
Everything could be won through me
So much I know already so much
I forget like the fly the dragonfly-dream.

Mitch Cohen

DURS GRÜNBEIN
1962–

Trilce, César

There were days it was all we could manage
    to say 'It may never happen' or
        'Something will turn up . . .' bored in

overheated libraries where, in moments
    before they completely glazed over
        our glances found themselves drifting
          like smoke-rings
        under the lofty coffered ceilings
          of Alexandrian reading-rooms.
        Most of us

    wanted to get away (to New York
    or someplace): we were students

with funny cracked voices
    enthusiastically turning
        failed projects in our heads, and some of us

        in melancholy anarchy
            were in thrall to new totems, idols
    of gone revolutions and the
multiply acupunctured body of magic.
    If you spent the whole day there
        (especially in winter),
            it was pretty cheap, alone
                between the short intervals

with our poste restante worries, owing
    for the rent, sucking the silence

from books like nerve gas
of all these mild beasts (. . .) and sometimes
even in the monotonous
hothouse climate there was a
somewhat living surprise
(Trilce, César!). I

remember one particular
summer afternoon
the rustling dusk
I was in the toilet taking a dump
when I heard rapid breathing
from another cubicle and an accelerating thumping
and I was alarmed as an entire
swarm of blowflies at the

love of two men silently belabouring
one another
sweating and oblivious like strange
centaur-like creatures on an

overexposed photograph.
Hard to forget
the relief with which,
with freshly combed hair
red faces and creamy complexions

they separately walked past me and only
a wink (a wink that went
through me) assured me:
they had gotten acquainted.

Michael Hofmann

All About You

A series of impenetrable instants
    jammed up together like
rumours by the light of an insistently
        ancestral politics, a

sequence of rapidly changing grue-
      somenesses, the moronic ping-pong
        chatter of a few newspaper-
readers on a park bench, and you
        you're just enjoying the calm

under a low sky
   (in the theatre opposite they're rehearsing
    Shakespeare . . . 'We
humanists . . .').

      You wait and then
      you choose your moment between
        the baby carriages
      and the flock of mangy pigeons that

fly up in a sort of *haute volée* gobbling –
      You can picture them
      with se-
    vered
   bloody heads in the gutter, a
  vivid daydream,

      the bespattered extras in an
      assassination flic ('The
Murder of Leo Trotsky') or the usual

BBBBB films . . . but instead you just
    gander on very slowly

to the next crossing, because
today is all about you.

Michael Hofmann

Untitled

A new poem began
on this foggy morning
of the anniversary of Garcia
Lorca's murder. Children
eating ices and old
men with strangely swollen
heads passed us on our
way to the registry office

where our cruise ship
was launched without any
of the usual waving and cheering
unblessed but for all that
still crewed by the evil
spirits of both families.

We had learned to span
silence quite effortlessly
in the evening like a taut
sinew: they couldn't see
what we felt like
as the targets were wiped.
Two small clouds
moved off in a westerly direction,
the city dyed the heavens
gray overhead and
I said I had enjoyed

wandering over the garbage
heaps with you. But you
were wearing those crazy
shoes: canary yellow, and
we were in a hurry as
a particularly cool drizzle
started to fall.

Michael Hofmann

MonoLogical Poem # 2

From time to time
I have these days when

I feel like embarking
on a poem again

of a kind that still isn't
all that popular. I mean

one without any meta-
physical refinements or

that thing that lately has stood in
for such . . . that type of

cynical genuflecting
at the stilted progress of history

or standing gasping akimbo
in the tough East-West marathon
as if you were one of

Alighieri's damned
with a stitch. Poems

someone said to me the other day

only attracted him if they
were full of surprises

written at those
odd times when

something still inchoate
a daydream a single

line begins somewhere and

undoes you.

Michael Hofmann

Titian's New Pad

Heaving with throw cushions. All the ornamental fish are
  yapping
Behind thickened glass, in water effervescing like Alka
  Seltzer.
Algae fan themselves with fresh blood. Peace returns to the
  aquarium,
At the expense of a few chewed up fins. The guppy stoutly
  dreams.
A pair of stockings plus garters is writhing at the foot of the
  sofa,
A portly cigar, with cummerbund, blows smoke rings from
  the massy ashtray.
Kilims, ankle-deep, unroll clear to the windows, like red
  carpets.
In golden palettes all over the apartment, glutinous colours
Are melting to the likeness of a rose, moon mountains,
  phlegmons –

Female nude here, Old Testament scene there. Three
    mirrors per glass-fronted cabinet
To cover your retreat into the labyrinth. Kickshaws on the
    mantelpiece,
Faience pottery and candelabra flatter the dependably
    childless denizens,
Smiling from framed photographs on tallboys, cruise snaps,
    captain and crew.
On the wireless someone with a nasty monastic cough is
    reading the Decameron,
Though only the afghan hound, blending in so nicely with
    the carpet tassels, seems to be attending.
'Shall I describe it to you, sweetness? The music of the
    spheres . . . Faked?
I suppose your orgasm was faked too? Don't take my word
    for it then, ask the fishes.'

Michael Hofmann

Lament of a Legionnaire
on Germanicus's Campaign along the River Elbe

There's nothing worse than this deadly retreat
following a battle, except the same retreat in prospect
weeks before . . .
Black as death the expression on the general's face,
the shambling, exhausted troops.
Behind the shields are the remnants of those unhurt,
footsore, running
with sweat. The incessant rain
has softened the tracks, the woods are one long ambush,
and the barbarians in packs, the wolves,
bite pieces out of our rearguard.
Whoever did not drown in the North Sea, far from home,

[193]

goes down in the swamps, as remote from the eternal city.
Over night morasses detain the whole legion,
by day it's rotten causeways, mouldering ladders,
from whose rungs a man slips to his death
with fingers crushed. This land merely punctuates fog
like some archipelago at sea . . . *Germania Magna*,
where the forests are still integral and dense,
no tree bobs on the sea cut to a bank of oars –
or a blazing hulk. The futility of fighting
over provinces as vast as continents, and territories
that can only be defended by further wars.
In the depths of the forest there is no triumph, and no Latin
    order.
And when, aged by many years, you finally make it home,
it will be to see the German installed under your lintel,
and waving to you your wife's tow-headed offspring.

Michael Hofmann

from Greetings from Oblivion City

Here a light breeze soughs through your memory every day.
Bears away singularities, keeps your conscience clear.
You stroll through life, bronzed, at ease. The shimmer
Of white teeth doesn't invite the visitor to eat,

Rather to forget. And the beach where seals consort
Is lined by palms, green pillars' colonnades.
In pastel villas live screen divas, ever young, of unimpaired
    allure.
Every cemetery breathes, like the soap in the comfort
    station, vanilla.

*

Even the (star-spangled) night sky is different here. Among the new
Constellations, glittering alongside the Lyre, the Swan, and Sagittarius,
Is a Sports car at full tilt, hounded by a Dinosaur.
Over the *Revolver* hangs the back-to-front *Baseball Cap*.

On the hills radio telescopes stretch out their flapping ears
For UFO and comet. People here will be quicker than elsewhere
To put out the welcome mat for little green visitors.
Cinemas here double as planetaria, and the odd bungalow

Houses an air traffic control center for the first space patrols.
At night, swivelling searchlights phase their beams in code.
Seen from the air, the city looks like a scrambled text anyway
That only beings with polyhedron eyes could ever crack.

The desert landing strips of the beaches are not for swimming off.
And taking a walk, you jump when a telephone shrills
On the promenade. No one around for miles . . .
A thrup from Mars pulses through the palms.

Michael Hofmann

LUTZ SEILER
1963–

good evening skip

what they love out here are their
threadbare little dogs. it's not
so far either
from sofa to fence
like it is in america. and at night
when the lights go out
high up in the treetops
a threadbare little shadow
presses up against the gate
saying:
they love me out here, take my word for it, love me

Susan Bernofsky

fin de siècle

i walked through snow with nervous
postwar whip lamps at my neck
across vienna's mozart bridge a tired
irish setter squatted there still
on a rope he

was dead and waiting for me that's
to say i untied the rope
from the railing's base began
to swing the creature round
& round a little skin and bone light
tolling bells blowing snow
started I sang

[196]

a little song about the danube back
'n' forth (I was a boy) the dead
setter circled now from my right
arm above the lovely
balustrade he wheeled
light & large into the nervous
postwar street lamp light a cut
grew deeper on his neck a whistling

got into gear his solid
eyes tiredly peeled
opened & shut: you

would have loved the mechanism of that look
and would have been still lonelier
about the snow, the bridge & the old song

Andrew Shields

'my birth year, sixty-three, that'

my birth year, sixty-three, that

infinite series of children, attached
to the hallways' echo vault, creeping
with a stoop into the pocket

of another, unfamiliar coat, seven
full of wax with a weight inhaled
in corridors, eight

with a weight that had arisen
from urinals to heads, we had
gagarin, but gagarin

[197]

also had us, every morning the same scraping
of sleeves pursuing writing
over the benches & at noon
the clockwork of spoons, we had

table duty, milk duty, the pressure
of an empty lesson in our eyes jelly
in the ears until
it fell silent
gravity fell silent
that was the pain
in our caps

while urinating, in the protective wood
while speaking, we had
quotations: at least we held a light
up against the planet's shadow sides
first all together & then
each of us again
silently for himself, we had

no luck. so the houses collapse
we finally become
small again &
ride back into the villages of wood, of
straw, from which we came, cracked & thin
with an echo sharpened

on the wind: we say hello to gagarin, we
have no luck, departure, back
to our villages
& departing the villages
across the fields at night . . .

Andrew Shields

now i lay me

before sleep a whispered conversation
with my mother's hairpiece I
cannot remember how

it sang from its pale
styrofoam head so softly
its lullabys loreleys sang

oh to be
twenty again & it told
me to sleep

Susan Bernofsky

MARCEL BAYER

1965–

Jihad Sounds of Home

They're playing jihad sounds of home
down in the courtyard, in the dark, like every
evening, the night sky keeps you awake.

They're playing the Cairo cassettes their
cousin brought them, you are with the
shadows, with yesterday, with the silence

of last night, you're thinking of certain
cookies, of sofas, you don't know why,
you're thinking of unmade beds, and you see

how the clouds shift, you're thinking
of blue-film dummies, you are with the
shadowy images, with soap flakes and

snow, while the sounds below
grow wild because their cousin sings
along the next time, his rough

voice in the courtyard, in front of the garage, it
carries all the way to the fifth floor, to the
sleeping quarters. It sticks in the youngest one's throat,

he no longer has command of such sounds. What
are the parents to do, whispering is
hard for them. I know nothing of their

gutturals: Yesterday was hours of glance-fear
and a numb feeling in my arm. Since then
the numbness has remained, or the doze

is coming. They play until almost seven, between
the houses it's already dawning, soon the child
will wake up crying, it knows no other

sound. They play until almost seven, then
the courtyard falls silent. On the street the
first cars, you pass into a light sleep.

Margitt Lehbert

Rapeseed

It's noon, you're sitting behind the wheel
on an empty country road, a couple of Polish stations
are cutting in and out, nothing speaks in you, you're on the
    point
of thinking you grew up mute, and then this: rape,

hard edge, clean line, scattered, dense rape work,
hatched and cross-hatched rape, the field fills, the screen
    fills
with rape, rape up to your hairline, brim full of rape,

rape eyes, rape head, rape rustle, rape scrape, nothing cattle
    cake,
nothing margerine, nothing but rape.

Michael Hofmann

VOLKER SIELAFF
1966–

Creation Myth

She takes a Kleenex
and wipes herself. The following gesture
is already borrowed
pre-programmed.

They were
certainly not tired, that much
should be understood. Maybe he just
stretched out beside her, under

the apple tree, or he went
looking for a cigarette, it's natural
to feel a little bit sad afterwards,
isn't that right?

I wouldn't mind
doing it again, she says, it's
so pretty here. I'm sure
no one can see us.

Hey, what's up?
I can't believe you're falling asleep on me,
when it was so nice
a moment ago!

Michael Hofmann

Sleepless

The racket of the birds
in the trees at a quarter
past three.

Cioran
complained of sleeplessness
all his life.

I
throw myself blindly
into the arms of the morning.

No experience
is communicable.

Michael Hofmann

HAUKE HÜCKSTÄDT
1969–

Liberation Square

In this square, called
liberation or friendship
that seems more like a foggy airfield
a mobile phone is the lowest
common denominator of hello.
Your number sounds like
an icecream van playing *Für Elise*
And if you pick up and speak
or breathe, I picture you
consulting the mirror

as you light up a Karo . . . Your voice
still does these abracadabra stunts
like a ribboning Super-8.
But any flashback
winds up in the same place
as the ladder in your tights.
Your eyes and mouth go dark,
instead of a sigh, the busy tone
a communication of sorts,
your diamond trump.

Michael Hofmann

Theme on a Variation

(Goldberg variation 25, recorded NYC, April/May 1981)

Gould sits on his stump of a stool,
in front of his Yamaha piano, and hums . . .
The position of head and hands
reminiscent of a toy-maker,
re-arranging the furniture in a doll's house,
shutting the windows after him.
April, the icebergs drifting past,
the room perceptibly brightened by them.
Over the silver dado rail
on the horizon, the picture of him
in the pose of an Eskimo
at the start of an expedition.
The walls so thin, you can hear birdsong,
clink of china, telephone conversations,
a train so very long that the level crossings
are simultaneously down in A and B.

Michael Hofmann

Going Beck

for A, two times

The morning was obscure and drippy,
all set to drench the sidewalks, the marquees, the garrets –
your bonzai Schwabing panorama.
In the beer-gardens, the chairs were sipping at the tables.
I took maps and trams, leaned on suitcases
or smiled at people, people with handicaps,
jobs, children, itineraries, crutches.

[205]

A withdrawn scout, seemingly reputable,
but with semen stains in his clapped-out pockets.
I really didn't want to wake up in someone's novel.
Pascal reckoned it was easier to describe
a pretty girl than a poem.
I retraced all my steps. Back on the train,
the rain thrashed against the windows.
Drops teared against the edge and hung trembling.
I took out my book which began with a man's dream
of slicing off his prick and burying it.

Michael Hofmann

No One Home

The room we lived in together
was deserted.

I hung around in front of the window –
a piece of wood getting in your light.

You were at one with the grandfather chair
in which I write these lines,

where you spent whole weeks muttering
litanies of human physical deficiencies to yourself:

Books cracked open and stimulating
like packets of prescription medicine or distalgesics.

Our halting intercourse
called to mind the injuries it was intended to treat.

In the morning, we conducted an autopsy on the wardrobe,
yanked open its doors, and reached

in among the small bones of the coathangers
where we dangled together.

Michael Hofmann

MATTHIAS GÖRITZ

1969–

For Volodya in Moscow

I go over to the window
and turn into a fine evening

What do people get up to in heaven?
If you die you're no longer in the world

In heaven they eat ice cream –
Or they will do if they have colour, at any rate

Is colour just a dreamspace
I'm in Mama's belly

God is making pizza there
When I get out, there'll be hell to pay

Mama yells
I say hello

I prefer not to imagine hell
I'm pretty sure it exists

Unlike a lot of things
Nothing is coloured white

My mothers are descended from apes
I'm sick of the sight of bananas

It all makes noise
And purgatory must be something like a chemical laundry

Everything in the world must die
And if we live on afterwards, for instance in heaven,

I bet it'll be raining

Michael Hofmann

JAN WAGNER
1971–

Frogs

From 1800 until his early death in 1810 the scientist Johann Wilhelm
Ritter – inspired by the discoveries of Luigi Galvani – undertook
numerous experiments on himself with the so-called Voltaic Pile.

the room – a chaos. what's not yet been sold
forms on the floor the scarcely decipherable formula

of his endeavour: wires, instruments
and books. empty bottles. his wife

is long since gone. and so is his last tooth:
'undeterred by respect for his own body' as achim

von arnim said, he battles with the wine
and with the premise that all life consists

of electricity. outside on the lake
it is suddenly uncannily still – the frogs are in secret

transmitting the new codeword to each other.

Georgina Paul

Acknowledgements

HANS ARP: 'Kaspar is Dead' translated by Christopher Middleton from *Modern German Poetry 1910–1960* (Grove Press, 1962), ed. Michael Hamburger and Christopher Middleton. INGEBORG BACHMAN: 'The Time Allotted' translated by Jerome Rothenberg from *New Young German Poets* (City Lights, 1959). KURT BARTSCH: 'Tears', 'G', 'A Visit from Enzenberger' and 'Question Answer Question' translated by Michael Hofmann. GOTTFRIED BENN: 'Morgue' (I, II), 'Express Train' translated by Michael Hamburger; 'The Evenings of Certain Lives' and 'People Met' translated by Christopher Middleton from *Primal Vision: Selected Writings of Gottfried Benn* (Marion Boyars, 1976), ed. E. B. Ashton; 'Night Café', 'Chopin', 'Little Sweet Face', 'Fragments', 'Blue Hour', 'Comme ci, comme ça', 'Listen' translated by Michael Hofmann. MARCEL BEYER: 'Rapeseed' translated by Michael Hofmann; 'Jihad Sounds of Home' translated by Margitt Lehbert (*Poetry Chicago*). JOHANNES BOBROWSKI: 'Trakl' translated by Michael Hamburger, used with kind permission of the translator; 'Childhood', 'Latvian Songs', 'Unsaid', 'Report', 'Mozart' translated by Ruth and Matthew Mead from *Shadow Lands* (Anvil, 1984), ed. Ruth and Matthew Mead. NICOLAS BORN: 'Market Position', 'Self Portrait' translated by Michael Hofmann. RAINER BRAMBACH: 'Morning', 'Single Men' translated by Michael Hofmann. VOLKER BRAUN: 'Oh Chicago! O Dialectic', 'Theatre of the Dead' translated by Michael Hofmann. BERTOLT BRECHT: 'A Cloud' translated by Derek Mahon, © The Gallery Press; 'Apfelbock or Lily of the Field', 'Ballad of the Love-Death', 'Pace of Refuge', 'To Those Born Later', 'Motto', 'Hollywood Elegies' translated by John Willett, 'Of Swimming in Lakes and Rivers' translated by Lesley Lendrum, 'Of Poor B.B.', 'Changing the Wheel', 'Reading a Late Greek Poet', 'And I always Thought' translated by Michael Hamburger, 'Thoughts on the Duration of Exile' translated by Christopher Middleton, '1940' translated by Sammy McLean, 'On Thinking about Hell' translated by Nicholas Jacobs, 'Of Sprinkling the Garden' translated by Patrick Bridgewater, 'The Solution' and 'Eight Years Ago' translated by Derek Bowman all from *Bertolt Brecht: Poems 1913–1956* (Methuen, 1976), edited by John Willett and Ralph Manheim. PAUL CELAN: 'Deathfugue', 'Tenebrae'; 'There was earth inside them' from *Selected Poems and Prose of Paul Celan* (Norton, 2001), translated by John Felstiner; 'Memory of France', 'Corona', 'Matière de Bretagne', 'Count the almonds' translated by Michael Hamburger from *Poems of Paul Celan* (Anvil, 1972). ROLF DIETER BRINKMAN: 'Landscape' translated by Michael Hofmann. GÜNTER EICH: 'Inventory', 'When the War was Over' from *German Poetry in Transition: 1945–1990*, translated by Charlotte Melin, © 1999,

University Press of New England; 'Report from a Spa', 'Brothers Grimm',
'Perspective from the Spezial-Keller', 'Some Tips from the Posthumous Papers',
'Confined to Bed' translated by Michael Hofmann. HANS MAGNUS
ENZENBERGER: 'In Memory of William Carlos Williams' translated by Reinhold
Grimm and Felix Pollak from *20th Century German Poetry*, Volume 69
(Continuum, 2001), ed. Reinhold Grimm and Irmgard Hunt; 'At Thirty-
three','The Holiday','Visiting Ingres' translated by Michael Hamburger from
Selected Poems of Hans Magnus Enzenberger (Bloodaxe 1994), used with kind
permission of the translator. ELKE ERB: 'Grimm's Fairytales', 'N's Identity'
from *Mountains in Berlin* (Burning Deck/Spectacular Diseases, 1995), selected
and translated by Rosmarie Waldrop. MATTHIAS GÖRITZ: 'For Volodya in
Moscow' translated by Michael Hofmann. GÜNTER GRASS: 'Folding Chairs', 'In
the Egg', 'Don't Turn Round', 'The Fortress Grows' from *Günter Grass: Selected
Poems 1956–1993* (Faber, 1999), translated by Michael Hamburger. GEORGE
GROSZ: 'Hymn to the World' translated by Michael Hofmann. DURS GRÜNBEIN:
'Trilce, César', 'All About You', 'Untitled', 'Monological Poem No. 2', 'Titian's
New Pad', 'Lament of a Legionnaire', 'Greetings from Oblivion City' translated
by Michael Hofmann. GEORG HEYM: 'Umbrae Vitae' translated by Christopher
Middleton from *Modern German Poetry 1910–1960* (Grove Press, 1962), ed.
Michael Hamburger and Christopher Middleton; 'Poet à la Mode', 'The Dead
Girl in the Water' from *Georg Heym: Poems* (Libris, 2004), translated and
inroduced by Antony Hasler. JAKOB VAN HODDIS: 'End of the World' translated
by Christopher Middleton from *Modern German Poetry 1910–1960* (Grove Press,
1962), edited by Michael Hamburger and Christopher Middleton. PETER
HUCHEL: 'Landscape Beyond Warsaw', 'Roads', 'The Poplars', 'The Garden of
Theophrastus', 'Psalm', 'The Mudcatchers' translated by Michael Hamburger
from *East German Poetry* (Carcanet, 1973), ed. Michael Hamburger, used with
permission of the translator. HAUKE HÜCKSTÄDT: 'Liberation Square', 'Theme
on a Variation', 'Going Beck', 'No One Home' translated by Michael Hofmann.
ERNST JANDL: from 'the big e' translated by Reinhold Grimm,
'oberflächenübersetung' and 'marking a turn' translated by Rosmarie Waldrop
from *Reft to Light* (Burning Deck/Spectacular Diseases, 2000). SARAH KIRSCH:
'Sad Day', 'Winter', 'Alone', 'Letter' translated © Wayne Kvam from
Conjurations (Ohio University Press). KARIN KIWUS: 'Hommes à Femme' from
German Poetry in Transition: 1945–1990, translated by Charlotte Melin, © 1999,
University Press of New England. PAUL KLEE: 'Water' from *Three Painter-Poets:
Arp/Schwitters/Klee* (Penguin Books, 1974), translated by Harriet Watts. UWE
KOLBE: 'Metamorphosis' translated by Mitch Cohen from *Berlin: Contemorary
Writing from East and West Berlin* (Bandanna Books, 1983), ed. Mitch Cohen.
HERTHA KRAFTNER: 'Inventory' from *German Poetry in Transition: 1945–1990*,
translated by Charlotte Melin, © 1999, University Press of New England.
MICHAEL KRÜGER: 'Footnote' and 'Ernst Meister in Memoriam' translated by
Richard Dove from *Diderot's Cat* (Carcanet). GÜNTER KUNERT: 'About Some
Who Survived' from *German Poetry in Transition: 1945–1990*, translated by

TRAKL: 'Eastern Front' translated by Christopher Middleton from *Selected Poems* (Jonathan Cape, 1968), ed. Christopher Middleton; 'The Rats', 'Psalm III', 'Grodek' from *George Trakl: Poems and Prose* (Libris 2001), translated by Alexander Stillmark, used by permission of the publisher; 'Childhood' translated by Michael Hofmann; 'Dream of Evil', 'De Profundis', 'Landscape' from *Translations of Song of the West: Selected Poems* (North Point, 1988), translated by Robert Firmage. JAN WAGNER: 'Frogs' translated by Georgina Paul from *Probebohrung in den Himmel* (Berlin Verlag 2001). FRANZ WERFEL: 'The Fat Man in the Mirror' translated by Robert Lowell from *Robert Lowell: Collected Poems* (Faber), ed. Frank Bidart and David Gewanter.

Index of Poets